Psychic Empaths and Narcissistic Abuse

A Survival Guide for Empaths to Understand the Narcissists Personality Disorder, Break Free, and Recover to Embrace and Improve the Development of their Gift

Diana Ortega

© **Copyright 2019 - All rights reserved.**

The content contained within this book may not be reproduced, duplicated or transmitted without direct written permission from the author or the publisher.

Under no circumstances will any blame or legal responsibility be held against the publisher, or author, for any damages, reparation, or monetary loss due to the information contained within this book, either directly or indirectly.

Legal Notice:

This book is copyright protected. It is only for personal use. You cannot amend, distribute, sell, use, quote or paraphrase any part, or the content within this book, without the consent of the author or publisher.

Disclaimer Notice:

Please note the information contained within this document is for educational and entertainment purposes only. All effort has been executed to present accurate, up to date, reliable, complete information. No warranties of any kind are declared or implied. Readers acknowledge that the author is not engaging in the rendering of legal, financial, medical or professional advice. The content within this book has been derived from various sources. Please consult a licensed professional before attempting any techniques outlined in this book.

By reading this document, the reader agrees that under no circumstances is the author responsible for any losses, direct or indirect, that are incurred as a result of the use of information contained within this document, including, but not limited to, errors, omissions, or inaccuracies.

Table of Contents

Psychic Empath Warrior

Introduction

Chapter 1: Are You A Psychic Empath?

    Qualities of a Psychic Empath

    Struggles of an Empath

Chapter 2: Types of Psychic Empaths

Chapter 3: Key Enemies of an Empath

    The Melodramatic Vampire

    The Victim Vampire

    The Narcissist Vampire

    The Intimidator Vampire

    Judgmental Vampire

    The Innocent or Unknowing Vampire

Signs of Emotional Exhaustion

Chapter 4: Thriving as a Psychic Empath

Chapter 5: Long-Term Survival Strategies

Chapter 6: Owning Your Superpowers

    Top Superpowers of Every Psychic Empath

    Using Your Superpowers to Impact the World

    Mistakes Stopping You from Exploring Your Superpowers

    Fine Tuning Your Psychic Abilities

Chapter 7: Common Myths That Psychic Empaths Should Never Believe

Conclusion

NARCISSISM AND NARCISSISTIC ABUSE RECOVERY

Introduction

What is a Narcissist?

A Relationship with a Narcissist

The Birth of a Narcissist

How Narcissists Choose Their Victims

The Cycle of Narcissistic Abuse

    Fundamentals of Narcissistic Abuse & Cognitive Dissonance

The Narcissists Arsenal

    Love bombing

    Manipulation

    Projection

    Language

    Cognitive dissonance

Narcissist's Language

Hardships of Escaping an Abusive Relationship

Breaking Free From a Narcissistic Partner: Strategies and Advice

Detachment

The Healing Process

Conclusion

Psychic Empath Warrior

A Survival Guide for Sensitive Empaths to Understand and Improve the Development of Their Psychic and Empathetic Abilities and Protect from Narcissists and Energy Vampires

Diana Ortega

Introduction

In psychology, empathy is a key component of being emotionally intelligent. In a world that is starting to appreciate emotional intelligence over the more traditional intelligence that is book smart, empathy counts as the main ingredient for improved social interactions. Empathy is defined in dictionaries and by psychologists as: the ability to understand and share in the thoughts and emotions of another person. In other terms, empathy entails putting yourself in another person's shoes so that you can understand where they are coming from and how they feel. It involves seeing the world from the perspective of another person so that you can appreciate their world, fears, struggles, and even joys much better.

Empathy is not the same thing as sympathy, even though most people will use the two terms interchangeably to refer to the same thing. While sympathy is mainly just pity, empathy involves going the extra step of trying to find a solution for someone's suffering. Sympathy says, "Oh, that's terrible, I feel so sorry for her" and then walks away, while empathy stays a bit longer in hopes that they can alleviate the pain at hand. Most human beings are born with the capacity to be empathetic. However, the extent to which this capacity is explored depends on the kind of nurturing that a person receives as they grow up.

So far, empathy does sound like a good thing. In fact, the world would be a better place if all of us were empathetic towards each other. There would be less judgment and less resentment. The world would be friendlier and a safe place where people's feelings and thoughts would be given equal priority, and nobody would feel unseen or unheard. Unfortunately, we do not live in an idealistic world where everything is perfect and flawless. We live among people who are capable of empathy, and also among others who consider empathy a weak concept. There is still another category of people who are completely incapable of being empathetic.

In our day to day lives, we demonstrate the ability to be empathetic towards others when we set aside time and energy to commiserate with their suffering. Even when we are best-intentioned, there are instances when we might not act in ways that are empathetic towards others. Other times, we might only feel some sympathy and then move along. This brings us to a slightly different category of people who demonstrate a more advanced form of empathy. These people are known as empaths.

An empath differs from an empathetic person in this way: while empathetic people are able to relate with other people's thoughts and emotions, empaths actually feel these emotions and thoughts as though they were their own. An empathetic person might relate to the pain of a colleague and then go on with their life. An empath will usually wallow in this pain because they feel it as if it is their own. A psychic empath is able to pick up another person's pain without necessarily being told. Their psychic ability allows them to tune into the suffering of another person even when this may not be so obvious to those who rely on verbal and visual cues.

There are different reasons why some people are empaths, while others only seem to experience moments when they are empathetic towards others. Nature is the first culprit in churning empaths. Some people are born with heightened sensitivity. You can see it in the way they respond to things, even when they are still small babies. They seem more alert and more attuned to their surroundings. The kind of nurturing that a person receives while they are growing up can also impact their development into an adult empath. If your sensitivity is honored for the gift that it is, you will likely grow up in the full glory of your empath self. On the other hand, experiencing trauma as a child has been shown to hinder a person's empathic abilities. Think of it this way —a child that is brought up in a caring and loving household has a better chance of becoming a caring and loving adult when she grows up.

If you are a psychic empath, you might have a very hard time going through the day since you are constantly surrounded by all this pain and suffering that you are aware of. It is important to learn how to shield yourself from emotional, mental, and physical drain while at the same time helping those who need your help. However, you must learn how to tell the difference between those who genuinely need your help and those who are only trying to take advantage of you.

In this book, you will learn everything you need to know to go from being a psychic empath to being a psychic empath *warrior*. A psychic empath warrior is one who harnesses their power to do good, instead of simply being at the mercy of their abilities and the energy of those around them. As a psychic warrior, you will have greater control over your emotions, and you will not go through life feeling overwhelmed and drained. You will learn to recognize the qualities that set you apart from the average person, how to identify energy vampires, and how to protect yourself from situations that will drain your energy. If you have always struggled to understand why you feel things the way you do, this book will act as a handbook that will make everything clearer.

The main objective of this book is to help you realize that what you have is a great gift that you can use to positively impacting the world and others while also taking good care of yourself.

Chapter 1: Are You A Psychic Empath?

Are you a psychic empath or are you just an empathetic person? Sometimes the line between these two can be blurry. Even the person who struggles with empathy sometimes has days when they really seem to feel other people's pain. This could be circumstantial. For instance, you are likely to feel more empathetic towards someone who is closer to you than a person you've just met. You may also extend empathy more easily if you've been through the same situation in the past. That being said, an empath definitely has qualities that stand out in relation to the way they share in other people's feelings of pain.

Unlike the average empathetic person who has their off days where they don't seem to care about anybody else but themselves, psychic empaths hardly have any downtime. They feel and sense energy right from the moment they wake up to the time they go to bed unless they know how to shield themselves.

There are some greatly distinguishing characteristics that set apart the psychic empath. These are elaborated in the section below:

Qualities of a Psychic Empath

You are aware of everything around and in you

The average person is often aware of what is going on in their life, at least to a reasonable extent. They can tell what they are thinking about, they are peripherally aware of what is happening in their external environment, and they are able to read the verbal and visual cues from the people they are surrounded by. A psychic empath takes this a notch higher. They can sense just about everything in themselves and their external environment. They are able to walk in a room and immediately read the mood of the room. They can tell when a person is getting angry or upset even before it shows on their face. If you are a psychic empath, you will find yourself being very aware of what is happening in your life and even in the lives of the people you care about. If a friend is going through a heartbreak, you will share their pain in a way that others cannot, even before your friend makes this pain public knowledge.

You hate crowds and prefer being alone

While you care a lot about people, you also prefer to interact with them on a one-on-one basis and not while they are in a crowd. You find crowds overwhelming and prefer to keep your own company. You like solitude because it allows you to recharge your energy. You cannot survive for long in a crowd setting. Crowds steal your joy; they make you nervous and anxious and they drain you. The reason why crowds drain you so easily is because you are constantly picking up energy signals from people and being in a crowd means you are bombarded with so many signals that you get overwhelmed. Do you prefer staying indoors to going out? Are you the kind of person who would rather watch a concert on TV than actually attend the concert in person?

You are an amazing listener

A downside of being known as a good listener is that people tend to take that as their cue to dump all their problems on you. If you have been suspecting all along that you are an empath, this is a problem that you likely have. Empaths are often keen to truly understand people and they do this by listening more than they talk. People love good listeners. Most people love talking about themselves and will gravitate towards anyone who gives them the chance. Because of your good listening abilities, you may have found yourself playing therapist to friends and strangers alike. Unfortunately for you, you might not have a whole lot of empaths in your life who return the favor. The journal you write in every night before you go to bed might be the only listening ear that you turn to after you have spent your entire day listening to other people rant about everything and anything.

You are highly emotional and often moody

An empath feels their emotions and then feels other people's emotions. Naturally, there is going to be a whole lot of moodiness going on. Imagine having to deal with the emotions of six people within an hour. How would that make you feel? Moody, at best and murderous at worst. This is the daily predicament of an empath. They may leave their house feeling all happy and content only to experience six different emotions even before they get to work. If you have a person in your life who seems to have a new emotion every hour, it might be that they are an empath whose feelings are linking with the emotions of other people. Do not judge them unfairly.

You often feel emotionally and mentally drained

As a psychic empath, it is natural to feel depleted at the end of the day when you have used up all the emotional, mental, and physical resources that are available to you. It can be especially daunting if you are working in a situation where you are constantly exposed to people who are in pain or who are upset. What makes it worse is that there are people who consciously drain your energy from you once they figure out that you are an empath. These people are referred to as energy vampires. Chapter 3 delves into the details of how to identify an energy vampire on top of sharing some simple tactics that you can employ to protect yourself when faced with an energy vampire.

Kids and animals naturally gravitate towards you

Kids and pets are not known to be articulate as far as communicating other people's intentions. However, they are both extremely intuitive. What young children and animals lack in communication skills they make up for in intuition. Intuition is defined as the ability to understand instinctively without relying on conscious reasoning. What this means is that a child will instinctively know that you are a good person without going through the steps of logical reasoning. The same case applies to pets. If you are the person that the dog runs to every time even though there are other people in the room, then maybe you need to start looking at yourself more differently. Especially if the other signs of the psychic empath as listed above already apply to you.

You struggle with intimate relationships

As an empath; it is common to struggle with the need to be loved while also wanting to be alone. Togetherness may not be your cup of tea, especially when this togetherness means being overloaded daily. Psychic empaths have to go through a wide range of emotions as they interact with people daily. When they are given a choice to be in a relationship or not, many psychic empaths want the opportunity to be alone just because it's so much easier than being with someone. It's not that they want to be alone forever; it's just that they have gone through the motions of being emotionally drained and they just don't feel like going through it again. It can be quite the delicate balancing act, and many times you will find yourself pushing people away. Some people may assume that you are simply scared of commitment without realizing that you are healing yourself from emotional scars and do not want to take any more on board.

Spirituality resonates with you

There are many different religions in the world with all sorts of rules and ideologies. However, all these strict rules of what you can and cannot do just don't make sense to you. When someone who is gifted with great intuition, they instinctively know what is morally right and wrong and abide their own natural laws that feel right to them. In today's world, the only concept that seems to make sense to the empath is spirituality. Spirituality is a wide concept, giving the empath a sense of freedom, encouraging a path of self-discovery, growth, and connectedness.

Spirituality also expresses the notion that we are apart of

something much bigger than this just this physical world. We are not a human having a physical experience. We are in fact, an eternal soul having a human experience. And this resonates well for the Empath as it ties in with their greater purpose of helping people in the physical world and increasing the Earth consciousness.

You love connecting with nature

Granted, many people love to admire the beauty of the natural world. For you, though, the connection feels deeper and more personal. You love to steal moments at the park, and your ideal home would be a cabin in the woods surrounded by the sights and sounds of the wild. Nature replenishes your energy. You love the greenery of trees, the ocean, and you love to spend your time hiking in the trails. You are never unhappy when you are out and about exploring the natural wonders of the Universe. After getting your energy sapped by those around you, you love the comfort of knowing that nature can restore this energy to the last bit.

You have been accused of being too nice

Empaths really do have hearts of gold. The problem with this is that they do not know when to stop pouring into others. If you are a psychic empath that will give the last shirt on your back, you probably have a few good friends who have picked up on the same. These are the friends who will accuse you of being too nice and tell you that you need to stop giving too much to people because they can see how much it drains you. What your friends may not know is that your generosity is ingrained in your DNA.

You have a very active mind

Most Empaths are quite introverted, which means they are in their head a lot. Thinking, observing, daydreaming, visualizing, reflecting and creating. Empaths view the world entirely different to the average person. This with their gifted intuition, comes a great edge, to create many amazing things to impact the world greatly.

However, this is usually restricted, especially in the empaths early journey from things such as lack of confidence, low self-worth, fear, doubt and uncertainty. Over time as the empath listens to their intuition and focuses on ridding these low vibrational qualities, life becomes exciting.

Struggles of an Empath

As an empath, you will likely have struggles that non-empaths cannot identify with. Simple situations that non-empaths can easily deal with (because they aren't using a whole lot of their emotional resources) will quickly drain you and leave you feeling overwhelmed. Empaths often find themselves struggling on a daily basis, and it can be even harder when you do not already know that you are an empath. As such, you might find yourself questioning why you tend to react in a particular manner when the people around you seem to take everything in their stride.

Mainstream media is overwhelming and draining

While most people look at television as a form of entertainment and a means to unwind after a long day, empaths often have quite the opposite outlook. Television shows can be exceptionally draining for an empath because of the myriad of emotions that producers and directors are aiming to elicit out of their audience. What's more, the news has turned into somewhat of a horror show in itself. Whether news anchors are reporting about the latest Middle East crisis or looming wars between dissenting countries, it only takes minutes before the empath starts their downward spiral into unpleasant emotions.

Empaths don't like saying no

Empaths also often struggle with saying no to others. Most people, empaths or not, do not like to say no to others. There is a certain struggle that comes with denying someone what they want, even when you know it's for the best. It is not for nothing that there are campaigns aimed at helping others know that "no" is a complete statement and answer on its own. When you say no to a person's request, there are often negative feelings that will come by as a result. There might be guilt and even resentment. Empaths hate dealing with negative feelings. They prefer to say "yes" because they like to make other people happy. At the same time, they do not want to deal with any negative emotions that might result from turning down a person's request because then they might be drained by these negative emotions. At the end of the day, empaths find themselves in a rather difficult position where they need to learn to create boundaries by saying no but also protect their energy by learning how to say no in the most tactful way possible.

Empaths struggle with crowds and group interactions

Imagine being able to pick up people's energies just by being in their presence. How would that make you feel? For a moment, it might be fun knowing that you can read someone without even needing to ask what they are feeling. After a while though, you will likely become overwhelmed to the point where you will no longer have any desire to know what a person is going through. This is the life of an empath on a daily basis. When they are out shopping in malls or enjoying a day at the beach, empaths can pick up all the energy around them. This would be fun if all this was positive energy but unfortunately, in most cases, it is not. As such, social situations that provide fun mingling opportunities for non-empaths end up being quite the opposite for them. Often, empaths will choose to retreat to their own solitude. As a result, they get labeled as loners or introverts when in fact they just want to be able to enjoy companionship without getting too overwhelmed.

Empaths are at high risk for addiction

What happens when an empath gets tired of feeling overwhelmed? They look for a way out. An empath who is tired of going through the rollercoaster of emotion and energy will look for something to soothe themselves and quiet the chaos with. In many cases, this ends up being a bad habit, which could eventually turn into an addiction. Many addicts are often empaths who were going through a period of pain and wound up on the wrong path. This is not to mean that all addicts are empaths though. It is important for the psychic empath to replace these bad addictions with 'positive addictions.' For example, learning how to play the guitar or working out at the gym.

Empaths have a hard time holding jobs

Another area that empaths struggle with is the area of employment. Anybody who has ever had a job will easily tell you that jobs are not always fun. There are days when you will show up simply because you need a paycheck. For empaths, this kind of tolerance for something that is not enjoyable might be hard to come by. It is especially daunting for an empath to work in a work environment that is toxic. As such, many empaths struggle to keep jobs and even when they do keep the jobs, they might have a hard time rising to the top. Most people who are non-empaths might find it easy to stay sane in a competitive and brutal workplace where throwing each other under the bus is the norm. However, an empath will struggle with the emotions that come about as a result of this behavior. Empaths will always be on the lookout for jobs that bring them joy and satisfaction. Given the state of the current world, there are not many jobs that suit these criteria and especially not in the corporate realm. As a result, you might find in your life hopping from job to job for reasons that do not make sense to you. Why can't you hold down a job? Blame your heightened sense of empathy. Working for yourself can be a great option for empaths.

Empaths are often tired

Do you often feel tired and fatigued? You just might be facing one of the many struggles of an empath. Many empaths feel exhausted at the end of the day because of the many emotions that they go through when interacting with others. You might find yourself wondering how tired a person who sits at a desk all day might possibly be. Truth is, the office empath will spend eight hours absorbing and dealing with the energy of thier colleagues, only to find themselves absolutely fatigued at the end of the day. When he/she goes home, this empath might find themselves in a space where they continue to absorb the energy of the people they share a home with. If these people are not emitting good energy, the empath will continue to get drained. This will continue even as they sleep (assuming they share a bed with someone), and in the morning they will wake up without the benefit of a refreshing night of sleep. It is easy to see that the empath goes through a never-ending cycle of emotional and mental drain. It can be particularly difficult to maintain a healthy balance of feeling and healing as an empath. If you are always taking on the emotions of others without prioritizing yourself, there is a high chance that you will burn yourself out.

Many people like to take advantage of empaths

Even when they do not mean to put themselves in that predicament, empaths often find themselves as the delegated dumping ground for all kinds of emotional garbage. Friends, family, colleagues and even strangers often use empaths as their platforms for unloading every emotional and mental baggage that they may have. Since empaths rarely say no (and are such good listeners), they are often left to mop up the mess left behind, while the other party moves on with the relief of having gotten something off their chest.

They struggle to articulate who or what they are

A lot of psychic empaths struggle with their self-identity. This is often a result of the conflicting, and often demeaning, messages that they have heard about themselves all their lives. When a psychic empath grows up in a household that they are not listened to or dismissed as being dramatic or too emotional, they retreat into a shell for protection purposes. In this shell, the psychic empath wonders about who they are.

Am I really just too emotional?

Am I being too dramatic? Am I overreacting?

Am I right in behaving in this manner or will I come off as being too sensitive?

What is wrong with being too sensitive anyway?

These are all questions that an empath might struggle with. Such questions breed self-doubt and self-doubt is often the root cause of low self-worth and identity issues, which are all struggles that empaths commonly face.

They may struggle with depression and anxiety

Because of the myriad emotions that psychic empath goes through, and the fact that they rarely get any support for it, there is a high chance for the development of depression and anxiety. Of course, this is not to say that psychic empaths are all depressed and anxious. The truth of the matter; however, is that psychic empaths are highly predisposed to depression and anxiety because they are essentially emotional sponges. They mop up emotional spills and keep them in. When these spills accumulate inside the empath with no healthy outlet, there is a significant risk for depression and other mood disorders.

They struggle with personal relationships

Imagine being able to pick up the feelings of everyone around you. How would this change your perception of relationships? You might be unwilling to get too close to people because you find them too much to handle. You might be unable to confront the feelings that you arouse in other people, especially when these feelings are those of discomfort, sadness, anger or even hate. In short, you might not do very well with getting close to people. Couple this with the fact that many empaths are introverted and live inside their heads and you have yourself a recipe that does not allow for very many personal or intimate relationships. While the empath may want to feel close and loved, they like their downtime a lot too. Striking a balance between being loved and being left alone is definitely something that many empaths struggle with.

Dealing with Narcissists

It is not uncommon for an empath to have experienced or dealt with a narcissist in their life. In most cases, it is either experienced by a narcissistic parent or narcissistic partner or both. As we know, empaths have supreme empathy. Narcissists, however, are incapable of expressing any signs of empathy. To the narcissist, people are viewed as objects that can be manipulated as if they were on a chess board in order to serve the narcissists very own needs. Empaths seem to find themselves entangled frequently in the narcissist's web of deception purely because it is so easy for the narcissist to manipulate them, especially if the empath is early in the process of self-discovery.

Overcoming narcissists, however, is a natural part of the process as we are able to recognize red flags much better in the future and ensure greater protection. They also reflect our weak points that we need to work on in order to become a more empowered individual. An empowered empath will not be susceptible to the manipulation and mind tactics of a narcissist.

Chapter 2: Types of Psychic Empaths

Psychic empaths are not all alike. There are different types of psychic empaths, depending on how they sense energy around them. The six different types of psychic empaths include the emotional empath, the claircognizant empath, the geomantic empath, the telepathic empath, the precognitive empath, and the psychometric empath.

Emotional Empath

This is the most common type of psychic empath. An emotional empath is able to pick up the emotions of the people around them very easily. They can feel the sadness of a sad person and the joy of a happy person as if those two emotions were their own. If an emotional empath is not self-aware and able to differentiate their feelings and those of others, then they can become emotionally drained very quickly. If you consider yourself an emotional empath, it is important that you learn to step back and take care of yourself so that you do not get mentally or emotionally drained.

Claircognizant Empath

Sometimes referred to as an intuitive empath, the claircognizant empath is able to read other people just by being in their presence. Claircognizant empaths are hard to lie to because they can recognize lies even though the person is trying their best to mask their intentions. If you are able to look at a person and immediately sense the energies of deceit around them then you just might be a claircognizant empath. If you are this type of empath, you will prefer to surround yourself with people who have good and clean energy that aligns with your own.

Besides being able to easily read people's intentions, you will know that you have claircognizance if you seem to experience coincidences more than the average person. For example, you might pick up your phone to call your best friend only for the phone to start ringing. The name on the caller ID? Your best friend. You also seem to be brimming with new and wonderful ideas that you cannot wait to share with others. Claircognizant empaths are often very artistic and creative. They make for very good musicians and writers because they can sense what other people want, and then articulate this perfectly.

Geomantic Empath

A geomantic empath has the ability to read and recognize the energies given off by the planet. In other words, they can communicate with the environment around them. How do you know if you are a geomantic empath? A key sign to look out for is when you feel a strong connection towards a place or if a particular place strongly repels you. It could be because you are picking up energy that you either like a lot or strongly resent from a particular place. Geomantic empaths tend to have the ability to tell when a natural disaster is oncoming. For instance, they might sense when a tsunami is on the way even before the meteorological department issues an alarm. Many animals tend to have geomantic empathy. They will, for instance, run and hide for cover before the onset of a tsunami.

Telepathic Empath

In the simplest terms, a telepathic empath is a mind reader. They can tell what is going on in another person's mind without needing to be told. A telepathic empath may also be able to read the needs of entities that are not in a position to communicate the same. For instance, plants and animals. This paranormal ability of the telepathic empath makes it possible for them to tell when someone is telling lies. They can easily read the lies as they tumble up and down the person's mind. It is important to note that a person may be a telepath and not necessarily an empath. Where these two concepts of telepathy and empathy intersect you have a telepathic empath. On its own telepathy is the ability to read minds. It is a concept that has been greatly argued, with an equal number of proponents and opponents.

Psychometric Empath

Psychometric empaths are able to pick up energy from inanimate objects such as clothing. They can tell the emotions and experiences that a person went through simply by touching an item of clothing previously worn by that person. If you have watched television shows about missing persons where psychics are contacted by the victim's family to try and find out what happened to that person, then you most likely have watched a psychometric empath at work.

How can you tell if you are a psychometric empath? You will know if you are a psychometric empath if you find yourself drawn or repelled by objects based on the energy they emit. While other people are able to go through life not bothered by things like chairs, scarves, cups and other inanimate objects, you will find yourself hating the presence of these things if they give off negative energy. Of course, this might not be the kind of thing that you will easily open up to people about. It might seem strange to a colleague to tell them that you dislike the energy that the coffee maker gives or that you are getting strange vibes from the photocopier. However, knowing that you are not going crazy and that psychometric empathy is indeed real should bring you some sense of comfort.

Precognitive Empath

A precognitive empath has the ability to experience an event before it happens. Often, this experience will be in the form of a premonition or a strong foreboding. Precognitive empaths experienced a sudden shift in mood or physical experience when they are undergoing these experiences. This could happen during waking hours or in a dream. If you have ever had a bad feeling that preceded a disaster or tragic event, then you experienced something that is referred to as precognition, which in other words is what a precognitive empath goes through on an almost daily basis. This gift can be used to predict and avert disaster, especially when the empath takes time to practice using their gift. This gift can also present itself positively. For example, you may get an insight into a place you will be traveling to in the future, or the arrival of a newborn baby in the family.

Chapter 3: Key Enemies of an Empath

If you ever encounter an energy vampire in your life, you will feel it even before you know it. How so? Energy vampires have a way of taking away all the good energy from other people's lives and replacing it with feelings of emotional drain. Some energy vampires do this deliberately, while others are unknowing about the destruction caused by their negative energy and presence. Regardless of whether an energy vampire is intentional or not, you must learn how to identify one and how to handle being around one.

Let's start by defining what an energy vampire is. An energy vampire is a person that feeds off other people's energy. Often, an energy vampire is an emotionally immature individual who is unable to feel their own energy voids and therefore looks to others for fulfillment. When a person that is emotionally mature and stable experiences certain feelings such as anger or sadness, they often try to process these feelings by themselves. Energy vampires do not have this capacity. Instead of sifting through their emotions, they project these onto others. In the process, they steal away all the good energy from others and replace it with their own emotions of anger, sadness, despair, and other negative feelings.

Dealing with an energy vampire can be extremely draining, especially when you are not aware of the fact that they are an energy vampire. There will be many times when you will wonder why you always feel a particular kind of way after spending time in the company of a certain individual. You might wonder whether you are being unfair and judging that person harshly. What you might not know is that you are right to feel that way because the person in question is an energy vampire who always manages to take you to the brink of emotional exhaustion.

Energy vampires come in different forms. Knowing how to tell them apart is the first step towards ensuring they are no longer capable of stealing your emotional resources from you. The main types of energy vampires, otherwise known as emotional vampires, are: the melodramatic vampire, the victim, the narcissist, the intimidator, judgmental, and the innocent vampires.

The Melodramatic Vampire

The melodramatic vampire feeds off drama. They cannot exist in a place where there is no drama. This kind of energy vampire thrives on blowing everything out of proportion and must always be the main character in every show. If you are in a relationship with this kind of person, you will always find yourself caught up in one public scene or another. Outbursts will be a common occurrence and you will often catch yourself in cringeworthy public encounters. Melodramatic vampires do not care who gets swept up in their wave of conflict and heightened emotion. They only care that they get the attention they want when they want it. At work, a melodramatic vampire might take the form of a colleague who is always making a big deal out of every little thing that they do. You will catch this colleague in the office kitchen and at the printer's complaining about how hard their life is because of one thing or another. You might even hear them whine on and on about how late they were in getting home because another colleague did something that inconvenienced them, however minor that might have been.

Why do melodramatic vampires behave this way? Most people who seek attention at whatever cost do so because it validates them. These are often the kind of people who, for one reason or the other, never learned how to be comfortable with their own selves without the need for external validation. This could be as a result of being neglected as a child or because they grew up believing the world revolves around them. Either way, the child may grow up thinking that they are owed attention and that the only way to feel whole is by making sure that the entire world is watching them.

If you are faced with a drama queen or a melodramatic energy vampire, the very first thing you need to know is this: you do not owe anybody your time or attention. They are very few people on this Earth that you are obliged to give your attention and time. Your children, for instance, rank highly on the list of people who can reasonably demand to be made a priority in your life. You are also worthy of the attention and time that you so effortlessly give to others. Outside of those two, you get to choose who gets your time and who gets cut off.

A good thing about people who love drama is that they are easy to spot. Soon after meeting a person, you will be able to tell whether they thrive on drama. You can spot it in the way they approach conflict and the way they carry themselves in public. If a person is always screaming and yelling and demanding to see the manager at every turn, run away and don't look back. This is the same sort of person that will burn the house and throw cooking pans at you because an old acquaintance texted you at ten o'clock at night, without first determining the reason for the text message.

If you are unable to walk away from someone that loves drama, for example, if it is a colleague or boss that you must work with, the important thing to remember is not to encourage their drama. Do not get tempted to participate in their shouting matches. Do not say things that feed their drama. As long as a melodramatic vampire is not getting anything in return, they will not be able to keep up their show for too long. The energy they seek will not be available for them to steal. In the case of a family member who is a drama vampire, limit the amount of time that you spend with them. Just because someone is related to you does not mean that they are allowed to get away with bad behavior.

The Victim Vampire

The victim is always easy to identify. They like to play the supporting role in every bad circumstance in their life. They do not take responsibility for anything and always have a finger ready to point at someone else. An energy vampire that takes on the role of a victim can be identified by their love for complaints and their complete lack of responsibility. In their world, nothing is ever their fault. Everyone else is to be blamed for their actions and they will complain about anything and everything under the sun. Oh, and don't even bother wasting your time trying to get an apology out of them. They feed off the pity that they elicit from others every time they share their woes. While it is important to be sympathetic to the suffering of others, you must be careful about the kind of attention that you show towards the victim. If you show too much sympathy, the victim will never leave you alone. They will always keep coming back in the hope that you will show them some of this sympathy that they have gotten used to. Unlike the drama vampire that you might easily cut off without a second thought, the victim might be harder to get rid of. This is simply because you might feel guilty about abandoning someone who is in need of your help but you must know that these people love to take advantage.

If the victim in your life is someone that you really care about, consider helping them set some goals in their life that can make them feel as if they are in control. Ensure that you put in place measures of accountability that will help determine whether they are being responsible and working towards their goals. For instance, if you have a sister that is always complaining about their finances, consider helping them to set up a savings or investment account. Have them contribute a portion of their paycheck to this account every month. By doing this, you will have changed the narrative from one of pity to one where the victim feels empowered to do something about their life.

Otherwise, if you have an energy vampire in your life that loves to whine about everything, does not take responsibility for their own actions and that you are not particularly invested in, feel free to cut them out of your life. Limit the amount of time you spend around them and you will begin to feel your energy levels peaking again.

The Narcissist Vampire

Narcissism is a personality disorder that is characterized by an inflated sense of self-importance, entitlement, and an obsession with one's physical appearance. Narcissists believe that they are the best thing since sliced bread and will often go to great lengths to prove this point. They do not take kindly to criticism, and they often do not care about what other people have to say unless it is said in admiration. Perhaps you've already encountered one of these types of energy vampires into your life since they love empaths.

Finding yourself in a relationship, be it romantic or work, with a narcissist can be one of the most daunting things you will ever go through. You will spend your life placating the ego of the narcissist and saying yes to all their demands, while your needs fall on deaf ears. A narcissist will steal all the joy and air from a room and then blame you for it. They will want to control every aspect of your life and make it their own domain.

Out of all energy vampires, the narcissist might be the most dangerous based on the lengths that they are willing to go to maintain the status quo. Because they are incapable of feeling empathy, the narcissist will not even care that you are facing emotional drain because of them. They simply cannot relate to your predicament however much you try to show them that you are getting beaten down by their negative energy.

When you find yourself faced with a person who exhibits the qualities of a narcissist vampire, the first thing you should do is consider the possibility of cutting them out of your life. This might be easy in some instances and harder in others. For instance, if you are just getting started on a romantic relationship and notice the signs of narcissism, it will be easier to leave because you are not invested. What happens when the signs start showing up four years into a marriage? It might be harder to just walk away. It is even harder when it is your boss who is the narcissistic vampire.

When dealing with a narcissistic boss, for instance, you will need to be very smart about your approach. One of the things you can do is make sure that you never allow them to get under your skin. Do not give the narcissist the satisfaction of knowing that they will always get a reaction out of you. This is what drives a narcissist—knowing that they can push you to the point where you explode. If you never explode, you will have denied them the ending that they so yearn for. Another way to protect yourself is to avoid argument so that you never give them a chance to twist your words against you. Narcissists will take advantage of every word that comes out of your mouth to ensure that they have the upper hand. As long as you do not say anything, you will have denied them the ammunition that they are so desperate to have.

Do not feel the pressure to massage your boss' ego just because they are a narcissist that thrives on it. It is tempting to play along with the narcissist just for the sake of keeping the peace. Many employees quickly learn that they can get favors from their boss by saying the things that their boss wants to hear. Always remember that you were hired because of the skills and value that you bring to the table, and you do not need to dance to the tune of your boss just because it makes him or her feel better when you do. It is not your job to appease the insecurities of your narcissistic boss because insecurities are in fact the root cause of the narcissist's behavior.

What happens then if the narcissist vampire in your life is someone that you love, or are romantically involved in, or maybe even a family member? Loving a narcissist can be very draining, especially because you often get nothing in return. Narcissists do not know how to love others. They love themselves and they love the things that other people do for them. They are also experts at wearing down the people who love them, mentally and emotionally so that they are never able to detect their manipulative ways.

If you are caught up in a relationship with a narcissist who is willing to change (and this is very rare), consider going into professional counseling and establishing boundaries that help you maintain a healthy union.

If the narcissistic vampire in your life is unwilling to change and is constantly abusive, walk away and do not look back. In many cases, abusive narcissists only get worse, so do not stick around hoping that things will get better. You will only be setting yourself up for failure if you refuse to prioritize your well-being, which is exactly what the narcissistic vampire is counting on.

For a more in depth guide on understanding narcissists and how to escape being in a relationship with a narcissist, you can check out my other book: *Narcissism and Narcissistic Abuse Recovery: Free Yourself by Understanding the Narcissists Personality Disorder, What the Hell Happened in Your Relationship, and How to Effectively Heal.*

The Intimidator Vampire

Have you ever met someone who behaved as if they had a point to prove? If you have answered yes to this question, then high chances are that you have encountered an intimidator vampire. Intimidator vampires have deep-seated insecurities that they constantly battle with. They feel weak, small, and intimidated by life and everything around them. They reiterate and compensate by trying to make the people around them feel these things in return. As such, they are hell-bent on making others look weak and inferior and unworthy. The intimidator vampire will often hold bigoted views on things, especially when this bigotry is shared within a group that makes him think he is better than he actually is. Such vampires are also racist and will commit hate crimes against others, especially while in groups.

The biggest identifier of an intimidator vampire is the fact that they are unable to hold their own when confronted. They thrive by hiding behind ridiculous beliefs and in numbers. They can never stand up in front of a group of people and say the things they do unless they have the backing of their fellow bigots. You will be able to spot an intimidator vampire based on their loudmouth and often obnoxious behavior.

When dealing with an intimidator vampire, the first thing you need to realize is that their attempt to make you feel inferior stems from their deep feelings of inferiority. They are not actually as aggressive and confident as they want to come across. In the confines and safety of their homes, intimidator vampires are like scared little cats that want a hug. However, it is not your job to give this level of comfort. Intimidator vampires could benefit from professional counseling so that they can confront their feelings of unworthiness. Another practical step to take when dealing with this vampire is to agree to disagree. Accept the fact that you can hold divergent views without getting in each other's faces about it. Do not try to argue with an intimidator vampire. They will beat you at it by being loud and saying the most outrageous things. Lastly, do not engage unless you absolutely have to. Whenever possible, walk away before things escalate. The intimidator vampire can especially say very hurtful things because they are looking to hurt those around them. If you do not want to get caught up in this, simply walk away and refuse to engage.

Judgmental Vampire

Why are some people so judgmental? You probably know a

few judgmental people in your life. They always have something to say about everything, even when nobody has asked for their opinion. They will pick apart other people's relationships, their choice of attire, their lifestyle choices, their career decisions and all of these will fall short. It is often impossible to please a judgmental person. Nothing you do will ever measure up to their standards. Having a judgmental spouse or parent can be particularly discouraging, especially when you are trying your best to be the best version of yourself.

So, again, why are some people so judgmental? To put it succinctly, judgment often comes about as a result of what is within a person, and less as a result of what is going on around them. It has been said that we hate most in others those things that remind us of ourselves. This is the driving force behind judgment. You may not even be conscious about it but the trauma that you experience will always be at the back of your mind guiding your emotions and turning you into the judgmental person that you said you'd never be.

Some people are often unable to separate the action from the doer, and as such will always have a finger to point even without understanding the context of the act. When this is coupled with a lack of empathy, it can be particularly difficult to be anything but judgmental.

If you have a judgmental vampire in your life, be careful not to take everything that they say personally. Understand that the jabs thrown your way may just be symptoms of some underlying hurt that the vampire is dealing with. This does not mean that you need to take everything lying down. Consider calling out the vampire on their behavior, but ever so sweetly so that it does not become a shouting match. Being firm and solid in your truth about who you are will also help to ensure that you are not overly affected by the criticism of other people. If all else fails, cut out the judgmental vampire from your life. Life is too short to stick around people who are always trying to put you down. Surround yourself with positive energy.

The Innocent or Unknowing Vampire

Some people drain us without meaning to. They simply come to us with their needs and problems because it is the only thing they know. Your children, for instance, will constantly turn to you for support and reassurance without being aware of the fact that they drain you or that you need someone to support and reassure you as well. Good friends may also be the unknowing vampires in your life if they are constantly looking to you to provide the emotional support that can only come from a friend.

With the innocent vampire, it is important to remember that one of the most effective ways of helping someone is by showing them how to solve their own problems. If your child is always coming to you with the same problem, show them how to solve it. Empower them so that they are less reliant on you. At the same time, learn to take some time out for yourself. Mothers, in particular, have this overwhelming sense of guilt every time they check out of parenting for a few hours to have some time for themselves. Motherhood is a tough job and to do well at it you will need to set aside moments where you focus solely on your self-care, unapologetically and with no guilt. When it comes to your friends, you will need to set boundaries and let them find their own wings as well. While it is great to be known as the friend that always shows up for others, you also need to show up for yourself. This is the only way you will remain in good form without feeling the effects of being drained by the unknowing vampires in your life.

Signs of Emotional Exhaustion

The thing about emotional exhaustion, otherwise known as emotional drain, is that it can often be disguised as something else. For example, you might experience emotional drain in the form of headaches. When this happens, you may be tempted to chalk it up to dehydration, exhaustion or just the everyday stress of your work. The fact is that emotional drain often creeps up on you, only for you to realize one day that you are completely and totally exhausted. You will try to look back and think back to when the emotional drain started, and you will likely be unable to pinpoint the exact moment. As an empath, you may sense another person's negative energy and the impact it has on you, and yet be unable to consciously recognize the cumulative effects of that energy. Just as you are sensitive to other people's needs and emotional states, you will also need to be aware of your own needs and the state of your emotional health. Look out for the signs of emotional drain and take appropriate measures before it spirals out of control.

Insomnia/ Difficulty Falling Asleep

Insomnia is perhaps one of the loudest signals of emotional exhaustion. When your mind is filled with stress and worries, it becomes almost impossible to fall asleep. The mind requires a certain state of calmness and relaxation so that it can settle into a state that is conducive for sleep. An emotionally exhausted person is at a place where all the emotion centers in their brain are fired up. They are like little flickering lights that refuse to go out, even when it's time for bed. Pay attention to insomnia when it comes calling. It is often a clear sign that something is wrong in your life.

Nobody stays up at night tossing and turning when they are emotionally healthy and happy in their life.

If you are having trouble sleeping, there are certain steps that you can take to make this a thing of the past. Of course, eliminating the stressors in your life (also known as energy vampires) should be your go-to step every time you catch yourself falling down the black hole that is emotional drain. However, we have so far determined that getting rid of energy vampires is not always possible depending on the type of relationship that we have with them. So, in the case of insomnia, there are several tips that you can apply to remedy the situation.

First, learn to switch off from your job when you leave the office. Do not carry the stresses of one place to the next place. By doing so, you will be allowing yourself to carry all the negative aura of the workplace environment and transfer it to your home, which should be your safe and happy place. Whenever possible, do not carry your work home. Many employees will lay awake at night worried about the pending report in their laptop without knowing that their emotional health supersedes the importance of that report. Seriously, leave work at work and enjoy your time at home. You are not what is holding the company together. Your report is not what will cause the company to come crashing down. Learn to take life in your own stride. If someone calls you after work hours for something related to work, make sure the phone call is brief and forget about the matter as soon as the conversation ends.

A relaxing bath infused with essential oils also does the trick when it comes to combating insomnia. Water is a friend to an empath. Water cleanses all the dirt and bad energy of an empath and leaves them feeling invigorated and ready for a peaceful night of restful sleep. Couple this with some chamomile tea and sleep meditation and you will be off to slumberland before you know it.

Lack of Motivation

When you started at your job, you were full of energy and ready to take on any assignments coming your way. Three months down the line, you are struggling to wake up for the very job you used to love. What changed? Well, you had several run-ins with your manager who happens to be a quintessential narcissist. This manager has managed to wear you down every step of the way. They criticize your work, put you down in front of others, and do not seem to have a single kind word to say about you. You have started struggling with your self-esteem and can feel your voice becoming quieter and quieter, where before it used to be bold and confident. A lack of motivation is a clear sign of emotional exhaustion. When you are constantly beat down emotionally it becomes almost impossible to be excited about things anymore.

You will know that your motivation has taken a hit when the things that used to excite you start to feel like chores. Because your emotional energy has been depleted, you have nothing left to give to the things that matter. Take a look around you. How is your living situation? Do you live in a clean house? Do you make your bed when you wake up? Can you honestly say that you treat yourself well by taking care of your hygiene, your health, your diet and anything else that relates to you? Were there days that you have treated yourself better? If yes, what changed? What are your goals in life? Do you see yourself putting in the conscious effort every day towards the achievement of these goals?

Taking stock of your current circumstances, and how much you have contributed to these, is a great first step towards determining whether you are motivated or not. Intrinsic motivation is a hallmark of an emotionally intelligent person. Emotional intelligence is a concept that an empath must learn if they are looking to manage those around them. The good news is that, as an empath, you already have the empathy part of emotional intelligence figured out. You only need to work on the other components, which include motivating yourself internally so that you really show up externally.

Anger and Irritability

When do you find yourself most irritable and likely to snap at the smallest things? More often than not, you will be prone to anger when you are going through a stressful event. When you are emotionally drained, you will not have the capacity for the patience that would be expected from a normal and logical person. Small things that you could previously have ignored will set you off and you will not be able to keep your cool in situations. Most people are smart enough to know that anger comes from a place of fear, hurt, and even frustration. These are all feelings that come about with emotional exhaustion. You'll never see a happy person lashing out at another. If you have been short-fused recently, consider evaluating whether you have also been going through a moment of emotional turmoil. You are probably not an angry person but simply a good person who got pushed too far and for too long.

Detachment

What happens to an empath who has been subjected to torrents of emotional abuse by the energy vampires in their life? They learn to steer clear, and with this steering clear comes a sense of detachment. Being pushed to the point of emotional drain is a type of trauma, and trauma often breeds coping strategies. Emotional detachment is a form of coping strategy. A person that is emotionally detached will struggle to form connections because they have unknowingly switched off their emotions to protect themselves.

Detachment could be towards people or even towards your own passions. You might find yourself feeling no desire or interest in a specific topic that previously excited you, simply because you are shielding yourself from the heartbreak and emotional fatigue of failure. You may also subconsciously choose to distance yourself from people because you have faced emotional exhaustion every time you get close to someone.

Pay attention any time you start to feel as if you are going numb where emotions are concerned. This is your wake-up call that something is not right. Nobody was meant to go through life not feeling any sense of joy or happiness from anything. If you catch yourself feeling numb and unexcitable about things, talk to someone. You might be totally drained and tired of putting up a fight. Professional help or even a kind listening ear just might give you the jumpstart you need to start feeling again. And remember, if the emotional drain that caused you to start feeling completely detached and numb comes from something that you do not have to have in your life, kick the stressor out. This includes your job. There is no paycheck on this Earth that is worth your emotional health.

Physical Pains

Emotional drain sometimes shows up in the form of physical pain. There are some tell-tale physical signs that suggest that someone is in the throes of burnout. These include constant inexplicable headaches or migraines and even dizziness. You might even start to experience shortness of breath and heart palpitations. All these physical symptoms point to an underlying problem of emotional fatigue and possible anxiety, which is both a symptom and a result of emotional drain. When faced with physical pain, your first stop should be your doctor's office. This will help you ascertain that there is nothing physically wrong with you. If that is the case, then you can move on to the next step of identifying all the energy vampires that have driven you to the point of emotional drain. Most doctors will not shy away from giving their honest assessment of the situation, especially when they realize that there is no physical cause for your symptoms. Many physicians are well aware of the tribulations that a lot of people go through in their everyday lives and are able to identify the symptoms of emotional drain from a mile off.

Lots of Crying

Granted, empaths are likely to cry a lot. There is always something waiting around the corner to tug at their heartstrings. It could be a cute video of a kitten or a baby taking their first steps and the empath will suddenly find themselves overcome with emotion. Being highly emotional is the empath's giveaway. However, if you suddenly find yourself bursting into tears in the middle of the day about nothing in particular, you might be going through emotional drain.

Crying is a good thing. A good well-timed cry can be extremely therapeutic. A happy cry, on the other hand, is always welcome and hardly makes anybody uncomfortable. However, if you are spontaneously crying in the middle of the day, in the subway, at work, during lunch or when you are printing your reports, then you might need to sit down and take stock of your emotional health. There is some science behind crying: when a human being is experiencing strong and overwhelming emotions, be that of sadness or joy, the limbic system picks up these emotions and sends a signal to the autonomic nervous system. In return, the nervous system activates the tear glands, or turns on the waterworks if you like, resulting in a good cry. An emotionally drained person is in a state of great emotional duress. They will go through their day experiencing extremely strong emotions because they are completely worn out. Your limbic system does not know that you are in the middle of a meeting, so it will simply pick up on these emotions and then send the necessary signals to the nervous system.

Hopelessness

A great singer once asked, where do broken hearts go? A good rejoinder to that question would be, where do hopeless minds go? Hope is the fire that keeps you moving even when you are not certain of how tomorrow will be. Can you feel that fire in your belly right now? If not, what happened to that fire? What took it away?

In the face of emotional exhaustion, it can be impossible to feel hopeful about anything. The mind is a powerful organ. In fact, the mind is the most powerful organ and tool that a human being possesses. In your mind, you can conceive ideas and decide what you want to be. You can overcome tribulations simply by telling your mind that you will. Many people have become great and left lasting legacies simply because they put their mind to it. There is nothing that you cannot do when your mind is in a good place. Hopelessness stems from a mind that is in a bad place. When your mind and emotion have been corrupted by the negative energies of energy vampires, you find yourself stuck with a vast plain of darkness and hopelessness. Everywhere you look seems bleak. Your dreams do not matter. Your suffering seems endless. You do not have hope that tomorrow will be better than today. You cannot see a way out. Narcissists are especially great at pushing their victims towards hopelessness because they know that this is a very effective way of shackling someone to their status quo. A narcissist vampire will constantly tell you that there is no life beyond your current circumstances. They will tell you that there is no better job than the one you have (if they are your boss) and that there is no one who could ever love you if you leave them (if they are your partner). The important thing is to recognize these statements as the blatant lies that they are. These lies are designed to get you feeling hopeless so that you can be easily worn down and made to do exactly as an energy vampire wants you to do.

Chapter 4: Thriving as a Psychic Empath

If you are an empath who wants to take back control in your life, you will be pleased to know that there are some short-term strategies that you can use. These are things that you can do in your everyday life, starting now, to feel better and be more in control of your energy.

Learn to Say No and Walk Away

One of the simplest tips to managing your energy field as an empath is learning to say "No" and walking away when negative energy enters your space. In your everyday life and interactions, there will be instances where you begin to feel your energy draining away. For instance, you might be in an environment where two argumentative colleagues are beginning to clutter your space with negative energy. At this point, it is best to walk away and remove yourself from that environment. It is important to do so without being apologetic. As an empath, you are often worried about offending other people. The problem with this type of mindset is that it puts you in unpleasant situations instead. When walking away from a toxic situation, do so without feeling the need to apologize and without worrying about who gets offended. Unapologetically protecting your energy is vital.

Just Breathe

At this point in the book, we have already determined that empaths tend to hate crowds. So, what happens when you find yourself in a situation where being part of a crowd is inevitable? If you cannot avoid a situation that calls for a gathering of a large group of people, then make sure you position yourself in a way where you are at the lowest risk of emotional drain. Standing in the center of a crowd only makes you highly vulnerable to energy drain from the energy vampires surrounding you from all sides. A safer position would be at the edge of the crowd, somewhere in a corner where some bits of you are partially hidden from the energy signals coming from the crowd.

Breathing deeply is yet another way an empath can deal with their emotions when they start to feel overwhelmed. A deep breath can center and ground you when you start to feel drained and bombarded by the different energy signals that you receive from those around you. A deep exhale from the mouth serves to expel the bad energy from within you, while an inhale through the nose replaces this with the clean energy from nature. Breathing in and out is also a meditation trick that is aimed at helping you become more conscious of your emotions. A deep breath can calm your nerves and get rid of anger in an instant. Next time someone is projecting their anger onto you, take a quick breath and allow yourself to feel the good energy taking center stage in your body.

Limit Physical Contact

As a psychic empath, you are able to receive the energy of the people around you through eye contact and even physical contact. This means that the more you touch and interact with people, the more likely you are to receive the energy that they have within them. As much as possible, limit the amount of physical contact that you allow in your life, at least until you are sure that you will not be receiving bad energy from a particular person. It is within your rights as a human being to refuse to give hugs to strangers or even particular friends and colleagues, especially if these individuals make you feel drained after every hug. Sometimes, even the most well-meaning people can drain your energy through physical contact if they are needy and constantly seeking physical affection and affirmation. Stay-at-home moms who spend all day with small kids who are constantly clawing at them to be picked up and tended to know how draining it can be to always be on the giving end for physical affection. At the end of the day, such moms only want to be left alone without any physical touch. Empaths tend to have the same problem when it comes to constant physical touch. In the same breath, reenergizing physical touch can be very powerful to the empath. An empath must; therefore, figure out the people who are great for hugging and those that must be avoided.

Make Time for Alone Time

Creating alone time is another crucial strategy that an empath must have if they are to survive living in a crowded world where escaping other people's energies is almost impossible. Alone time is one of the best ways to fully recharge and get ready to face another day for the empath. During this alone time, you may choose to do whatever makes you happy. You can read a book or watch a wholesome movie. You can even take a nap or soak in a bubble bath. The only person who can make the rules of alone time is you, depending on what you like best. However, the key thing to take into consideration is that alone time with your smartphone does not count as alone time. The smartphone is one of the top enemies of an empath. Not only do smartphones interfere with the ability to sleep thanks to their blue light, they are also awash with depressing information and social media trolls who rank highly as energy vampires. Always remember to put your phone onto airplane mode before going into alone time. Calls and text messages should not be answered, while you are enjoying your solitude. Any emails that come through during your moment of peace must remain unanswered. Learning to switch off and just bask in the quiet is one of the greatest gifts you will ever give yourself as an empath.

Say Goodbye to TV and Facebook

Another great tactic that will help in your survival as an empath is switching off the television and staying off the Internet. The television and the Internet are both great channels for accessing information. Unfortunately, they are often filled with a lot of negative energy that can be debilitating for the empath that soaks everything in. While it might be beneficial to watch television and access the Internet every once in a while, it is very easy to over-consume irrelevant information and going overboard is only going to wear you down. A good way to go about this is to set aside time for accessing the internet and TV. This allows you to monitor the kind of information that is being sent your way and put an end to things when you start to feel drained. Staying off social media is also a good idea. Facebook, Instagram, Snapchat and other social media platforms help us stay connected to our friends and family but are also highly detrimental when abused. If you are able to call the people you love on the phone and talk to them, then there really is no need to have numerous social media pages that expose you to the negativity of the online community.

Prioritize Yourself

As an empath, it is normal and natural to always put the needs of others ahead of yours. You are born to be a giver. It is part of who you are. In fact, giving is the essence of who you are. To survive in a world that is almost always taking without giving anything in return you will need to learn how to be selfish. It is ok to put yourself first. In fact, according to airline safety instructions you are supposed to put on the oxygen mask first before attempting to help others. In everyday life, this means that you should always take care of yourself first before taking care of others. This makes perfect sense as you cannot pour from an empty cup. Train yourself to prioritize yourself first. It is ok to worry about yourself first and to care about yourself first before caring about the next person. You might feel guilty for a while, but you will soon realize that you are in a better position to give to others when you give to yourself first.

Visualization for Protection

Visualization is the art of taking your mind on an adventure. Instead of just thinking about your current environment, visualization allows you to remove yourself from that state and think of something much better. A good way to utilize visualization in protecting your energy is to imagine yourself encased by an impenetrable shield that protects you from all the negative energy of the world. You could even visualize a fierce lioness guarding your personal space and running off all energy vampires. This technique comes in handy when you suddenly realize you are in the presence of an energy vampire, especially the innocent vampire. With the innocent vampire, you may be halfway into a conversation before you realize how invested you are and how drained you feel. This is a perfect time to use visualization to protect and regain your energy and stop fully investing in the conversation.

Be Grateful for Your Gift

Empathy is a great thing. It is not a burden that you have been cursed with. Being an empath is a great gift that has been bestowed on you so that you can heal yourself and others. When you are in the trenches dealing with heavy emotions, empathy can feel like the worst thing to have. You might have days when you wish you weren't capable of feeling as you do. There will be moments when you will be envious of your less empathetic friends, and their ability to shrug off things and events as if they did not happen. Even in these moments, remember that you are greatly blessed and highly gifted. Gratitude is a good way to train your mind to see your empathy as a good thing rather than a heavy burden. Psychologists have studied the human mind and found that being grateful has a way of lifting depressed spirits. In fact, people who are often dealing with depression are told to write down three things that they are grateful for every day. After several weeks of consistently expressing gratitude, most people report happier and lighter spirits. If your spirit is heavy about the fact that you are an empath, consider keeping a notebook where you can write down three things that you are grateful for every day. It could be the fact that your intuition saved you from doing something or how you were able to lift someone else's spirits at work. Either way, you will soon start to realize that what you have is a good thing that should be cherished, regardless of how it feels on some days.

Consume Positive Material

Being an empath can be challenging at times and the quickest path to becoming a psychic empath warrior is to indulge in the world of self-development. Whilst there is an overwhelming amount of useless information out there, there is also a plethora of incredible knowledge out there in the form of books and audiobooks. A book can be a worthwhile companion when you are struggling with an unruly mind because it engages your attention on a new set of ideas or skills for you to learn. And even if you do not like reading, you can still indulge in a good audiobook on your commute to or from work. Audiobooks are especially great in ensuring that you do not get lost in your own thoughts, as you have someone right there reading to you, ensuring you do not tune out and go to that quiet place that empaths love to retreat to. As you continue to learn new information over time, you will be surprised at how much of an impact this will have on your life.

Chapter 5: Long-Term Survival Strategies

As an empath, you will need long-term survival strategies that will help you cope with living in a world that is highly demanding and full of negative energy without getting overwhelmed. Unlike the shorter-term strategies that were discussed in Chapter 4, the long-term strategies will require a little bit of practice and persistence. Incorporating these strategies in your everyday life will help you become a better person who can take care of themselves and impact the world around you without losing yourself. And don't worry, some people might say that you are changing, that you are becoming more selfish and inaccessible or that they do not know who you are anymore. Do not take these statements too seriously. Part of growth is discarding the old bits about us that no longer work for us and bringing onboard new tactics that help us become the best versions of ourselves.

Define Your Needs as a Person

One of the very first things you will need to do is define what your needs and desires are as a human being. Every person has what they believe to be their purpose and objective in life. For instance, your current purpose and objective might be to be the best mother to your child. Maybe you are set on accomplishing various milestones as an employee and getting ahead in your career. Your objective could be simply to be as happy and satisfied as is humanly possible. The most important thing to do is to be clear on what this very essential need is in your life. Remember you are allowed to have multiple needs and categorize all of them as a priority. Now the next thing after identifying your needs is to determine the things that you require in order to meet these needs. For instance, a mother who wants to do the best by their child might require a supportive partner in order to be able to balance the demands of parenting and having a career. Such a mom will be uncompromising in their choice of partner. They will not allow a partner that is non-supportive and energy-sapping anywhere near them. This is because they have already defined and have a clear picture of what their needs are.

This type of mindset can also apply to the workplace. If you haven't determined what you need and what you won't stand for, you will often find yourself surrounded by the same energy vampires that you're trying your best to avoid. Defining your needs as an employee will help you determine what company to work for in terms of company culture, career progression, and compensation needs among others. A common problem that empaths have is not knowing when to speak up. As long as you know what your needs are, you will be in a position to speak up. When you are pushed to the wall you will be very clear about what is happening and take steps to change the situation because you are already familiar with your needs.

Take out a notebook right now and make a list of the things that you want from life. Take time to search your soul and figure out exactly what you would want from life if it was up to you. Now take a step back and realize that it is all up to you. Only you can determine what you get from life depending on the things you allow to happen. Use your notebook of needs and desires to remind yourself of what you are hoping to get out of life every time you start to feel muddled or depleted. If someone is responsible for making you feel muddled or depleted, remind yourself that this person is not acting in the best interest of your needs and then remove them from your life.

Stamp Boundaries in Your Life

In the beginning, empaths are known to have very weak boundaries and is something the empath must consciously work on to improve. Defining your needs will bring you to the very crucial second step of stamping boundaries and limits. Stamping boundaries in your life allows others to recognize what you will tolerate and what you won't tolerate. When you have boundaries, you teach other people how to treat you.

Many of the people that you initially meet do not know how to treat you and rely on the cues you give them to make sense of for themselves. Sure enough, there are some written common decency rules that govern social interactions. For instance, it is rude to ask out a woman when she is out and about with her husband. Almost everybody knows this. Those who do not yet know this will soon find out and in a very unpleasant manner. However, there are other personal rules that you might have that people do not know of. Let's say for instance that you have set aside an hour before bedtime to meditate. The colleagues you work with do not know this, so they keep calling you long after you've left the office to discuss work. Some of them call while you are in the middle of meditation. Meditation is your safe place and your time to recharge. Instead of being upset about your colleagues calling and keeping quiet about it, setting boundaries would look like this: Your colleague calls right before bedtime, you refuse to pick the call. The next morning you let them politely know that your evenings are set aside for family time and personal time. Chances are that they will not be calling you after work anymore.

Boundaries do not just apply to colleagues. You have to set boundaries with your family and friends too. While most of us love our friends and families, it is important to recognize that they can also be very draining in their demands. When faced with an empath, some friends and family can take and take until there's nothing left to take. As an empath, you need to recognize that you can love someone and still say "no" to them if saying "yes" would be detrimental to you. Whether we are talking about saying yes every time a family member needs someone to babysit or saying yes to requests for funds and soft loans, you must be careful to draw the boundaries where they belong. After a while, people will realize that there are things that you will not allow in your life and will stop asking for favors at every turn. By doing this, you will be able to live a much happier life as you are in control of how you want to live your life and not letting others control you.

Take Note of the Energy Drainers and Energizers

In order to favorably impose your boundaries and limits, it will be essential to define the energy drainers and energizers in your life. Just as there are energy vampires that take away from you, there are people and situations that serve to boost your energy and morale. As a sensitive person, your energizers are assets that must be guarded. Long walks, alone time, communing with nature, and quality time spent with someone who truly loves you are all examples of energizers that an empath will benefit from. Once you know what steals your joy and what adds to it, you will be able to draw the lines regarding where each of them fits in your life.

Balance Your Chakras

Do you know what chakras are? According to Indian spiritual thought, chakras are the energy points that every human being is born with. Every person has a total of seven chakras, which begin right at the start of the spine and go all the way up to the top of the head. The seven chakras are responsible for reenergizing you in various aspects of your life. For instance, the solar plexus chakra, also known as Manipura, is what gives you your self-identity and confidence. If your solar plexus chakra is underactive, you will struggle to make sense of who you are and even lack in self-esteem. If it is overactive, you might end up being egotistical or arrogant. Whether you ascribe to these beliefs or not, it is important to acknowledge that the premise of the chakras is one that makes total sense. As human beings, we are not just empty vessels that come to be and then complete our journeys in mortality. There is a driving force behind our actions and our lives. As an empath, it is important to ensure that you balance your chakras (or whatever you may prefer to call them) so that you can have a balanced life.

There are several simple tips that you can apply in your life to ensure that you awaken your chakras to help you be the best version of yourself. Walking barefoot, for instance, is known to connect you with the earth in what is known as grounding. In spiritual circles, grounding is the connection that happens between yourself as a spiritual person and the earth with all its energy. Grounding allows you to release all the bad energy that is pent up inside of you while getting some good energy from the earth in return. The chakra responsible for keeping you grounded to the energy of the earth is known as the root chakra. Grounding is vital for empaths who find themselves stuck in their head too much overthinking and overanalyzing.

Getting a relaxing massage and dancing are other ways you can fire up your chakras and heal yourself if you have been feeling a bit overwhelmed. If you do not have the time or opportunity for either, soak yourself in a warm bath complete with bath salts. Epsom salts combined with lavender oil make for a very relaxing and energizing bath that will have you feeling reborn and completely balanced. While you are soaking in your bath, call positive thoughts into your mind by repeating affirmations such as *I am loved, I am safe, I am strong.*

Strengthen Your Mind with Positive Affirmations

Speaking of affirmations, that's another thing that you will need to learn as a long-term strategy if you wish to take control of your life as an empath. Positive affirmations serve to reinforce the empath's subconscious mind of who they truly are, what they believe and how they want to live their life.

For every one, as a young child, the subconscious mind is like a sponge. No matter what is in the environment, positive or negative, favorable or unfavorable, the sub-conscious mind will absorb it. So whatever negative traits and beliefs your parents have, it is most likely you picked up these unwanted traits and beliefs. And for the sensitive empath, the chances of absorbing these unfavorable beliefs and traits are much higher.

This is why self-awareness is so important, because we are able to observe the unwanted and make a conscious effort to remove this and reprogram our subconscious mind. Through the use of repetitive positive affirmations over a long period of time we are able to rewire the subconscious mind to create a much more desirable life, and can then help others to do the same.

Positive affirmations can be anything that you want them to be, as long as they are positive and encourage you to be your best self.

Example of positive affirmations that you can work with include:

I am an empowered empath.

I am a calm and peaceful person.

I am smart and make sensible decisions.

I have the strength and wisdom to change my life.

I am not a prisoner of my mistakes.

I attract wealth and abundance into my life.

I surround myself with positive and uplifting energy.

Another thing to note with positive affirmations is that you can also use them to bring something into your life that you do not currently have but want to bring to your life. However, when you affirm this desirable thing, you must bring it into the present moment by speaking as if you already have it.

You do not want to affirm "I want." By affirming "I want" you are emitting the vibration "I want" and are only going to receive back the vibration of "I want" therefore, you will never truly manifest this desire. By emitting the vibration "I am" or "I have" that is the vibration you will receive and ultimately how you manifest what you truly desire, by affirming as if you already have it.

For example, let's say you desire a black Range Rover.

You would affirm: "I drive a beautiful black Range Rover."

And as you affirm this desire, use the power of visualization and truly feel yourself gripping the steering wheel of the Black Range Rover with the brown leather interior driving down the road. Feel yourself in the moment.

A great example of a positive manifestation is Jim Carey writing himself a check for 10 million dollars to himself dated 10 years into the future, keeping it in his wallet. And after almost 10 years was up, he discovered that he was going to earn 10 million dollars for acting in the movie Dumb and Dumber. Amazing!

Make a list of the things that you want to affirm and attract right now and then use them as your affirmations to strengthen your mind and your reality. I would recommend then getting yourself an affirmation journal, so you have something organized to write down and store all your affirmations. You can go through your affirmations either first thing in the morning or right before you go to bed.

Express Gratitude

What would be a great addition right next to your affirmation journal is a gratitude journal. Affirmations and expressing gratitude tie in very well together and I recommend filling out both journals together. Let me explain why.

While you are a person that carries an impressive and admirable ability to detect other people's pain and bring them healing, you must always remember that you are the vessel through which the power of the universe flows. Remaining humble in the face of the gift that you have been bestowed with is a great way of ensuring that this gift continues to flourish. Arrogance has been known to stand in the way of many success stories. Do not let yours be one of them. Always take a few minutes of your time every day to express gratitude for what you are capable of doing. Expressing gratitude in your life serves two purposes. One is that it helps you to start seeing your ability as the gift that it is, and not as a burden that you have been yoked with. The second purpose gratitude serves is that when you vibrate on the frequency of gratitude, you will receive more things in your life to be grateful for, as that is the vibration you are emitting.

Here are some examples of gratitude statements to get your mind ticking:

I am grateful for the existence and experience of life.

I am grateful for my health.

I am grateful for my friends and family.

I am grateful for my shelter, clothing, food, and water.

I am grateful for the internet and being able to connect with my friend across the world.

I am grateful for my beautiful pets. They bring me so much joy to my life.

Can you already see the power of practicing gratitude? After hearing these statements of gratitude your mind already starts to feel more positive and you start to feel good about yourself. So many people complain and focus on what they DO NOT have and continue to vibrate on the frequency of lack! And what do you think they continue to receive…? More Lack!

Gratitude is extremely powerful and highly recommend your practice it if you want to change your life in a positive way.

Just like the affirmation journal, I would suggest investing in a gratitude journal, so you have something neat and organized to fill out daily, either first thing in the morning or just before you go to sleep. This will keep you accountable and you will be able to reflect back in time and notice the changes this simple activity has had on your life.

Listen to your Body!

It is not difficult for an Empath to be in tune with their body. They know when a meal makes them feel good and they know when a meal makes them feel ill. The problem is when you choose to ignore this feeling. Despite being able to be in tune with their body if they want to, empaths are susceptible to using food as an escape from their stressful life. However, doing this for a long period of time will only lead to shame and guilt so it is important to stay in tune with your body and only eat what makes you feel good after. Yes, the oily Chinese meal may taste good at the time, but you know immediately after you're going to feel like crap after and regret it.

If you are always eating fast food, you will have a harder time getting in touch with your inner and best self compared to someone who chooses to eat a well-balanced diet of protein, low-GI carbohydrates, and healthy fats. Respect all three macronutrients as each plays an important role in serving the body.

Additionally, make sure you get plenty of water to drink. Water flushes out toxins from the body and leaves you feeling hydrated and refreshed. The benefits of water can even be seen on the skin. You can go from breakout-prone skin to glowing skin in a matter of weeks if you keep up your water intake. If water can do such wonders to the skin (which is visible for all to see), imagine what it does on the inside. Water cleanses you from the inside out. It is no wonder that most empaths love water. Whether they are drinking it, swimming in it or taking a bath, most empaths swear by the cleansing and healing powers of water.

Meditation and Yoga

Pencil in meditation in your schedule and you will begin to notice yourself becoming more aware of your emotional and mental states. Meditation helps you to get rid of the clutter in your life while channeling in the good energy and focusing on the positive. A great thing about meditation is that there are numerous resources that are available on the Internet at no cost that can help you get better at meditating. You may choose to access YouTube channels that are dedicated to meditation or even download meditation apps from the app stores. Whichever way you go about it, you will soon notice that you will have an increased boost of energy and will feel calmer, more relaxed, and less irritable.

Yoga also serves a somewhat similar purpose. Having been in existence for over five thousand years, Yoga has been used mainly as a way of connecting to the higher power of the Universe. The original purpose of Yoga was to promote self-awareness and discernment in individuals and make them see where they stood in the overall big picture of the Universe.

Create Your Safe Place

This is probably the most important strategy the empath can implement in their life. Every empath requires a place that is free from the everyday distractions where they can retreat and recharge at the end of the day and be alone with their thoughts. It is important that you create a physical space where you feel absolutely safe and where you do not have to interact with anybody that you don't want to. Your safe place could be your own bedroom or even a restaurant that has a corner booth where you can hide away from everybody else. While in your safe place, make sure you switch off your cell phone and your mind as well so that the worries of the external world do not interrupt your moment of relaxation. Bring a notepad and pen with you and write down your thoughts, ideas, goals, and ambitions.

Chapter 6: Owning Your Superpowers

Being an empath does not have to be a fight against constant suffering and emotional drain. As an empath, you have a powerful gift that you can harness to make the world a better place. The ability to sense energy is not something that everyone has. As a matter of fact, research has shown that only approximately 20% of the world are labeled as highly sensitive, a label under which empaths loosely fall.

Furthermore, approximately 3% of the entire population qualifies as having a psychic empathic ability. What this means is that you are a minority in the world, but you can still use your talents to impact the rest of the world in a big way. Sometimes you do a lot just by focusing on those closest to you. Someone smart once said; be the change you wish to see in the world. As you make the conscious effort to work on your weaknesses and become the best version of yourself, you unconsciously give others permission to do the same.

Top Superpowers of Every Psychic Empath

You are probably wondering whether the only thing you will ever be good at is sensing emotion and feeling the pain of others. On the surface, it can seem as if this is all there is to a psychic empath. Fortunately, this is not the case. Empaths are gifted with great superpowers that they can use to do good in the world. If this comes as a surprise to you, then it is probably because you have been riddled with self-doubt unable to notice the amazing sides to your gift. Let's explore the superpowers of the psychic empath.

The Superpower of Vision and Discernment

When a psychic empath settles their mind and learns to work through the clutter of their everyday life, they can achieve a vision that normal people are not capable of. This is because such an empath is able to sift through the chaff and pick out the important details. Empaths have a three-sixty degree view on things, and for this reason, they can make extraordinarily visionary and discerning leaders. Of course, such an empath will also have to work through their typical lack of enthusiasm for leadership roles. When a willing empath takes on a leadership role, there is often a change for the better. They can read the people that they are leading well, anticipate their needs and put in place measures to cater for these needs. Because they are excellent listeners, empaths make people feel heard and listened to, which is a key quality of an exemplary leader.

The Superpower of Advanced Intuition

While other people struggle to hear their gut instinct clearly, the empath's intuition leaves nothing to chance; it is loud, clear and demands to be heard. In many cases, the only reason why an empath might fail to side with their intuition is because they chose to ignore it, not because it did not show up when required. A psychic empath's intuition is like a well-trained army with red flags that are hoisted every time there is approaching danger. This army works tirelessly and nonstop. A psychic empath that allows their army to flourish will easily tell you that your new partner is no good for you, even when you think you are head over heels in love with this person. Just by looking at a person, an empath can tell when that person has good intentions or otherwise. Empaths who trust their advanced intuition are able to avoid a whole lot of dangerous situations.

Additionally, the psychic empath can also use their advanced intuition when it comes to making tough decisions. They are able to use this gift to vividly sift through the array of options that are presented to them and ultimately determine which particular option resonates with them best.

The Superpower of Psychic Ability

Seeing that this book is called *Psychic Empath Warrior*, it would be improper for the empath's superpower of psychic ability to be missing from this list. The empath's psychic ability allows them to see things before they happen or even when they are happening even though they can be separated by thousands of miles from the actual event. An empath's psychic ability will allow them to feel the pain of a loved one who is undergoing a hurtful situation thousands of miles away. Have you ever caught yourself thinking about someone out of the blue and when you call them, they let you know that they were going through a tough time? This could be because of your psychic ability. Your nature as an empath will keep you connected to this person who is continents away, while your psychic ability enables you to receive signals, in the same way, that a distraught person might send SOS messages in the hope of being rescued. Further down in this chapter, there is a detailed exploration of the things that you can incorporate in your daily life to develop your psychic ability and make it better than it already is.

The Superpower of Healing

Whether they are healing by speaking life into others or just by surrounding others by their calm presence, empaths have quite an impact when it comes to alleviating the suffering of others. As an empath who has learned to steady themselves, your mere presence can be a healing balm to others. You only need to show up, and everyone else feels at ease. You probably know one or two of such people in your life. Their presence makes you feel safe and comfortable as if everything in the universe is aligned as it should be. If you do not know anybody like that, it just might be that you are that person. You might unknowingly be the calming presence in people's lives. What a great superpower to have, to be able to meet with a friend for coffee, fully understand the problem they are experiencing, and offer them helpful solutions. Of course, the important thing to remember with this superpower is that you must heal yourself first. You cannot fix other people's wounds when yours are bleeding.

The Superpower of Creativity

Empaths are highly talented and creative. It only makes sense—you cannot be so highly gifted and fail to make something out of it. Many empaths go on to create music that lasts generations, make art that wows the entire world for years, or write novels that captivate millions of people. It is rare to find an empath who does not have a creative bone in their body. Creativity is the empath's outlet. Creativity is the empath's chance to pour their souls out without being judged for it. Think about it: the empath who has had to battle their emotions, otherwise referred to as demons, all their life often needs a safe space where he or she can express exactly what they feel. This empath will turn to a platform such as painting, singing, exercising, drawing, film-making, writing and any other creative outlet that allows for freedom of expression. It is no wonder that a lot of creatives come up with concepts that have everyone else wondering why nobody thought of that before. It is simply because the mind of an empath is like a never-ending maze with surprises at every corner. The well of creativity that an empath embodies can never run dry. And the best part is that the empath feels their art. The art comes from deep down within them, and at the same time mirrors the emotions of the people around them because the empath is able to be selfless in their art.

Using Your Superpowers to Impact the World

When used correctly, the superpowers of an empath have the ability to change lives. Whether at work or in personal relationships, an empath's intuitive capability is their greatest asset. As an empath, you have something that many people struggle to have: the ability to read a situation instantly without needing to ask questions. Coupled with the superpowers discussed before, it's easy to see that empaths have a lot of potential to impact people and communities everywhere they go. The obvious question, therefore, becomes, how does an empath go about the process of channeling their superpowers towards the right causes? In other words, how can you take advantage of what you have to improve your life and those of others?

Creative Direction

Because of their highly intuitive nature, empaths often come in handy when it comes to offering creative direction in work projects and even in their own lives. Creativity is never usually the direct result of pure logic. For art to appeal to its audience, there has to be an element of intuitiveness and heartfelt emotion. That is why some of the most celebrated authors of all time are usually those who write with a lot of sadness. They are able to draw emotions from their readers because they feel and understand these emotions.

Ernest Hemingway, a world-famous American journalist and writer, once put it aptly this way: *"There's nothing to writing. All you do is sit down at a typewriter and bleed."* In this statement,

Hemingway was recognizing the thankless labor that is writing and at the same time appreciating that the magic of art cannot exist without feeling or emotion.

As an empath working in the creative industry, you should never shy away from sharing your opinions and views on projects. Some of them might seem outlandish or ridiculous but it is often the bold empath who is willing to wear their creative heart on their sleeve that wins the day and inspires others.

Nurturing Relationships

Psychic empaths make terrific friends. They are excellent listeners. They are empathetic. They anticipate other people's needs. They are often nurturing and rarely judgmental. One psychic empath friend is worth ten in the bush, so to speak. When a psychic empath meets a well-meaning person with whom they are able to nurture a respectful and mutually beneficial relationship, their friendship blossoms for years and years. It is indeed a thing to be proud of if you are an empath because you can be such a great friend to the people who need you.

Empaths are not just nurturing to their friends. They extend this trait to their colleagues as well. Work environments can often be ridden with anxiety and other forms of toxicity. For someone who is not attuned to or who is unable to understand this negative energy, such work environments can be very distressing. Empaths can filter through different types of energy and obtain important insights which allow them to navigate any environment mindfully. As such, empaths are likely to make thoughtful colleagues who think before they leap and who try to understand where others are coming before judging harshly.

Besides friendships and work relationships, empaths also thrive as parents. Empath parents often have so much positive energy, encouragement, and empowerment to pour into their children. After all, an empath understands what ails their child even when the child isn't in a position to articulate it. As an empath, whether you choose to have biological kids or adopt kids who need a home, there is a strong chance that you'll be one of those parents who grow up to become best friends with their children.

Mediation Roles

Because they are able to understand people without requiring words to be said, empaths often make great mediators in conflict resolution. Their ability to detect problems before they escalate into bigger issues allows the empath to be one step ahead in times of conflict. At the same time, they are also able to dig deep into a person's psyche and understand their greatest needs and wants, and thus realign the mediation exercise to do the same thing, which ensures that all parties feel like they've been listened to.

Activists and Advocates

As an empath, you have the potential to advocate for the unseen and the unheard because you are able to see and hear them. An empath's deep connection with their surrounding enables them to have a heightened understanding of issues. While some people will litter and shrug it off, an empath will find it highly disconcerting to go about life with such an obvious disregard for others and especially for the environment. It is, therefore, not uncommon to find many empaths involving themselves in advocacy roles such as fighting against environmental pollution, being activists for human and animal rights, and even helping to bring the marginalized to the forefront. In the eyes of the empath, social injustices cannot and must never be ignored.

What's even better is that empaths are able to connect easily with people, and thus influencing people to join worthy causes comes naturally to them. When an empath pleads their case, it's almost impossible to ignore.

Career Choices

The best careers for empaths are those that allow them to live out their full potential as healers and caregivers without burdening them unfairly with emotional and mental drain. If an empath decides to go down a more draining path, but still feels fulfilled in doing what they do, it's important for them to learn how to take care of themselves so they are not worn out on a constant basis. In careers where an empath is constantly exposed to the suffering of others or high levels of drama and negativity, it's highly crucial that the empath develops healthy coping and protecting mechanisms to avoid emotional drain.

There are certain careers that are better suited for empaths for several reasons. Empaths, for instance, make very good artists. As mentioned earlier, they are able to feel deeply and this gives them a creative edge over everyone else. A wise person once said that life imitates art. By choosing to become an artist, an empath is essentially lighting a torch to show the rest of the world how to live. A great advantage of being an artist is that you don't even need to show your face to the rest of the world. You can allow your art to communicate on your behalf while protecting yourself from public attention, which can often be overwhelming. An artist who has chosen this approach is Banksy. Banksy, now 45-years old and based in England, has managed to influence the world with his art while maintaining his anonymity. His debut as a street artist was back in the 1990s and to date, nobody has been able to unveil his real identity.

Freelance writing and travel blogging are two other career choices that are ideal for the empath who wants to explore their creative side, impact people, move freely, and recharge their minds and bodies while keeping human interaction to a minimum. To be clear, this isn't to say that empaths hate working with people. Rather, empaths thrive more and make better use of their superpowers when they work in environments that allow their vulnerable sides to flourish without negative energy.

As an empath, you may also consider becoming an online coach or therapist. In both cases, you will be helping others and because there are guidelines to the kind of care you need to provide, you are able to help others while also safeguarding yourself. Other examples of safe and fulfilling career routes for empaths include charity, social work, and healthcare, especially mental healthcare. Empaths also make great veterinarians since they are able to deeply care for animals.

Overall, empaths do well in self-employment and in professions where they are able to help others. When an empath is in a profession that is a perfect match for their personality, they leave a tremendous impact that resonates with everyone they come into contact with.

As an empath, you may have previously struggled with holding down a job. It is important to recognize that this may be because you had chosen the wrong kind of job, or intuitively, your soul was trying to tell you that there is something else out there much better suited you. Something your soul is craving to express. With the right career, you can change lives.

Another path to consider as an empath is an entrepreneurship. This may sound daunting at first but let's break it down on why this is a good idea. Being an entrepreneur provides a great sense of freedom, which all empaths love. You set your own rules and your own work schedule. You are not bound by the limitations of having a boss. You do not need to ask for permission when to take a vacation or when to go to the bathroom. Additionally, in the field of entrepreneurship, you must know what the market wants. You must be able to provide to the market with something they are happy with. Something that is going to solve their problem. This is where the empath is truly able to shine. Using their ultimate gift of empathy, they are able to truly dive into the mind of the market and truly understand their pains and problems. And with this, can deliver a product to the market that satisfies greatly. Entrepreneurship also acts as a medium where the empath can unleash their creativity and come up with ideas and solutions, bringing great joy to the empath.

The worst careers for empaths include those which require one to be aggressive and competitive, deal with crowds, interact with a lot of people, and play by rules which are sometimes unreasonable or even unscrupulous. Professions such a politics, sales, and public relations don't suit most empaths.

Detecting Manipulation

An empath's ability to sense a person's negative energy even when the person is trying to disguise it as something else allows them to tell when a person is lying, even though everyone else may be in the dark. An empath who has learned to understand other people's energies without getting drawn into them is able to sense subtle energy shifts which may point towards potential manipulation. Manipulators use the same book of tricks including using body language and eye contact to create rapport with the intent of creating an aura of harmlessness. For the inexperienced eye, this kind of rapport may come across as genuine. Fortunately for empaths, inauthenticity is often detected from a mile away.

This ability allows empaths to protect themselves and those around them from predators who may be looking to take advantage. Since time immemorial, children have been implored to listen to their mothers since "mothers know best." The reason for this is that mothers are highly intuitive towards their children and are therefore able to predict danger even before the children can sense it. That is why your well-meaning mother might take one look at a girlfriend or boyfriend that you have just introduced to her and tell you that you're about to get into trouble. This kind of sixth sense that mothers have towards their offspring is the same that empaths have towards most people and situations.

Diffusing Negative Energy

The energy of an empath is light and positive by nature. When they're overwhelmed by other people's negative energies, empaths tend to be the light in the darkness. Just by being present in a place, an empath can make people experience lightness and positivity that starkly contrasts the energy that is often emitted by predators.

Even if you're shy to talk to people and hate crowded settings, you can use your mere presence to make others feel better.

Sometimes, words aren't even required. There is so much negative energy in the world that it makes all the difference if one person can be that lighthouse in the dark that shows those stranded in the dark sea that there is hope in the horizon.

Mistakes Stopping You from Exploring Your Superpowers

The unfortunate thing about the empath's superpowers is that they rarely get used. A lot of the time, empaths do not even realize that they are so incredibly gifted. And when they do, there are empaths who choose to have nothing to do with their superpowers. Why is this so? Why are many empaths afraid to unleash their full potential? There are several mistakes that are committed knowingly and unknowingly by an empath that stand in the way of their superpowers.

Wanting to Fit In

The desire to fit in causes many empaths to hide their powers behind curtains where nobody can find them. Truth be told, being an empath is not easy. You will not always feel normal. You might come off as a bit weird or even crazy. An empath who is aware of their power and realizes that they might be judged for it might choose to hide behind normal. You must remember that there is nothing interesting about normal. If you were meant to be normal, you would not have been gifted as you are. Different is good. Weird is good. You only need to learn how to embrace these weird parts of you. It is indeed true that nobody can make you feel inferior without your permission. If the world sees that you are comfortable in who you are, you can bet that there will not be many people calling you weird. And even if they do, the joke is on them because you have all these superpowers and they don't!

Thinking You're Too Much

You have grown up hearing the word *too emotional, too sensitive, too dramatic,* and *too much* used in relation to you and because of this you have decided that you are indeed too much to handle. If you show up in the world when you have already written yourself off, then the rest of the world will follow suit. You are not too much of anything. You are exactly what you were born to be. The shoes you wear are huge and not many people would dare to step in them. Embrace yourself for the masterpiece that you are, and instead of thinking that you are too much let those who are able to handle you stay in your life. Anybody else is welcome to leave just as they came. Remember that you have surmounted emotional labor that would easily break others. You fight emotional battles every day and come out unscarred. How dare you call yourself anything other than a hero!

Lacking Confidence

The way you speak, the way you walk, how you dress yourself up every morning before getting to work...these are things that can impact how good you feel about yourself, and how others perceive you. Of course, confidence is deeper than the Gucci belt on your waist, or the Ray-Ban designer sunglasses protecting your eyes as you sunbathe. Most empaths are introverts; introverts are not always known for speaking their minds. An empath might even choose to keep quiet for the sake of keeping the peace and avoiding confrontation. You've got to remember that the signals you send out into the world are the very same signals that the world will judge you by. If you come across as the shrinking violet, you will always and forever be that. However overwhelming you find crowds to be, you can still let your presence be known. A well-spoken and firmly articulate word in the middle of a meeting will allow you to share your creative self with your colleagues. It does not have to be a ten-minute explanation or justification that wears you down and gets you fighting negative energy from the opposing seniors. You only need to make sure that you believe in yourself, and that other people know that, and let them know that they have a reason to believe in you too. Most people have a way of taking advantage of the guy with no confidence—they make this person the doormat who is used and discarded at pleasure. Do not be this person.

Neglecting Physical Well-being

As an empath, it is typical to focus on getting the emotional bits healed while you neglect everything else. This makes sense seeing that emotions make up a huge part of the empath's life. However, it is important that you work on your physical body as well. Your mind will only work well when it is inside of a healthy body. Yoga, swimming, weight-lifting, and other low impact exercises can turn around your physical health and develop into a real passion that you can put energy into. You need to find a physical outlet for all the pent up tension and emotion in your body. What's more, physical exercise releases endorphins and dopamine, the feel-good hormones, which will have you feeling happier and refreshed in no time. If you do not believe that physical exercise does indeed make the empath happier, try one boxing class at your local gym. Imagining that the punching bag is your insufferable boss will have you rejoicing in the relief of revenge and you will not have to be so uptight around your boss next time they try to rile you. This does not mean that violence is ever the answer but every once in a while, you need to punch something that will not cry, if only to let out some of that steam that many empaths walk around with.

Forgetting to Laugh

Not everything needs to be serious in an empath's life. The emotional load that you carry is serious enough, so why burden yourself with the constant need to be serious? Learning to laugh at yourself is one of the greatest things that you can do for yourself. There will be days when your psychic ability will be off, and others when unusual coincidences will show up at your door. Take it all at your own stride. Being a psychic empath is not an excuse to go about life with a sour look on your face. You can be an empath and still have fun with it. Train yourself to see the funny side of everyday life and you will have the right kind of wrinkles. Laughter is referred to as the best medicine because of its ability to lift even the lowest of spirits. If you can find something to laugh about every day, then you will have moments in your day when you are not worried about other people's energy or emotions.

Refusing to Jump In

While the empath often encourages others to go in the direction of their dreams, the same does not apply to self-talk. Many empaths will spend hours analyzing why they need to be doing one thing and not the other. This is how the empath misses out on the best adventures of their life as they overthink. If your intuition has given you the green light to proceed with something, do not hesitate. Do it. You do not have to mull over the matter with your logical mind. If you do so you will only find yourself in an inescapable rabbit hole that is full of excuses as to why you should not do a particular thing. At the end of the day, your story becomes full of what-ifs instead of one full of great memories. Learn to jump in and see what happens—whether it is a relationship, a career, moving to a new place. The worst thing that can happen is that you will not like it, which only means that you will have to reconsider but at least you will have tried and gained new knowledge.

Fine Tuning Your Psychic Abilities

So far, the bulk of this book has been about getting you in the right mental and emotional frame to be the best version of your psychic empath self. Being right in your mind and in your emotions is the starting point to success in life, whether you are talking about being good at psychic empathy or anything else under the sun. You can only do right in the world if you do right by yourself. Now, after getting yourself well-grounded and self-aware of your abilities you might begin to wonder how you can be better at who you are. After all, aren't some psychic empaths so good at what they do that they become national heroes who go on to change the world? Wouldn't you want to be such a great empath that you are called upon to impact the world in a positive way? While not every psychic gets to reach the pinnacle of their paranormal ability, you are capable of developing your psychic abilities to get better at who you are.

Journal

While in the process of walking through the somewhat confusing maze that is the life of a psychic empath, you will accumulate lots of information that you need to process through. This information may be collected through conversations that you have with others or even via dreams. Either way, you will need to keep track of these little bits of information and in a way that does not clutter your mind. The best way to do this is by keeping a journal. If you had a strange dream about someone, write this down in your journal. You will have a detailed account to refer to when the events of the dream come to play out in real life. Journaling will also help you identify patterns of your psychic ability. Perhaps you will notice that you tend to have these strange dreams after talking to a particular person or visiting a specific place.

Befriend Other Psychic Empaths

One problem associated with being a psychic empath is that there is no professional organization of psychic empaths that meet once every year for networking purposes. It is common to feel alone and isolated as a psychic empath, but the good news is that you have kindred spirits in the world. You only need to know where to find them. A psychic empath who spends his or her days worn out by the energy of people around them will do well to surround themselves with people who understand exactly what they go through. A good place to get started on your search for kindred spirits is at your local spirituality classes. If there are no classes near where you live, you can still look up spiritual development circles and events in your region. Packing your bags and retreating to the mountains for a week of spiritual healing, awakening, and connection is worth the several months of clarity and fortitude that you will have after interacting with people who are like you. You may also come out of such events with lifelong friends and even mentors.

If you are still not able to find any sort of groups around your region there are plenty of Facebook Groups for empaths that offer tremendous amounts of value and help.

Develop Your On and Off Switch

One of the things you'll quickly appreciate as your psychic abilities develop is your control over them. It is important that you remain in control of your abilities so that they do not rule over your life. Having an on and off switch, so to speak, is important in ensuring that you are not in psychic mode at all times. You can develop your on and off switch by visualizing something that you need to do before and after engaging your psychic abilities. It could be something as simple as imagining yourself walking down a hallway and pushing a door open and then closing it afterward when you are done.

Maintain a High Vibration

Everything on earth has its own energy and from this energy comes the vibration. Your vibration changes depending on your thoughts and moods. A person that is negative, jealous, and critical will have dense energy that vibrates lowly. A cheerful and positive person, on the other hand, will have light energy that vibrates fast, thus drawing positive people to them. When people say that they do not like the vibe that a certain person gives off, it is correct to take this literally. Some people just have bad vibes, while others have good ones. Low vibration brought on by dark energy will attract its own kind, while high vibration will do the same. If you wish to tune into your psychic abilities, you will need to ensure that you are vibrating at higher frequencies than the average person. What you have is a special gift and you cannot afford to vibrate like the common person in the street. To attract the high energy that will help you become better at being psychic, you must be willing to emit this energy.

There are several things you can do to ensure that you set your vibration at a higher frequency than everybody else. To start with, you can simply train your mind to be more positive and to see the good side of everything so that you are not constantly weighed down by dark thoughts. Being out in nature and opening your heart to love is another way of ensuring you are always carrying the good energy that you need and deserve. Children and pets are especially great at giving the unadulterated kind of love that every psychic empath could benefit from. If you have a pet, spend a few moments every day where you just cuddle them and enjoy the closeness of this beautiful creature that loves you without demanding anything in return. This is going to perk your spirits right up, and high spirits equal high vibrations.

Watch what you eat as well. If you are always binging on high-sugar and high-carb processed foods, you will likely find yourself lacking in the good energy that comes from wholesome foods. Fruits and vegetables are especially great foods that will help you stock up on the good energy that you need. Fruits and vegetables absorb energy from the sun and transfer this energy to us when we eat them.

If you have always enjoyed getting a natural tan, now you have another reason why basking in the sun is even more important. It is not for no reason that the sun remains a revered source of energy, dating as far back as ancient cultures. The goodness of the sun goes beyond warming our skins and giving us important vitamins for bone development. Absorbing some of the sun's goodness is bound to leave you feeling energized and ready to vibrate on a higher frequency. Make sure that you protect yourself by not staying in the sun for too long as you do not want to burn your skin.

Silence the Noise

Your sixth sense is strongest when your mind is quiet and peaceful. The proverbial voice in your head that stops you from making stupid decisions is often your third eye trying to show you that the path you're taking is dangerous. Unfortunately, while being persistent in its means to communicate awareness, your sixth sense is also very measured in its tone. In the presence of noise and clutter, you'll not be able to hear a thing. So, learn how to cultivate silence in order to give your sixth sense a chance to be heard. Whether you're meditating, taking a walk or enjoying a lap or two in the swimming pool, train your mind to be quiet. Pause and take a breath and only then will you be able to hear the whispers of your sixth sense.

Cultivate Creativity

The rational mind is an enemy of the third eye. The rational mind often defeats the sixth sense with logic. Rationalizing things is often what causes people to make bad decisions even when their sixth sense is screaming for them to stop. To combat this problem, consider nurturing your creative side. In creativity, your imaginative side takes over from your rational side. Creativity doesn't require you to be perfect or logical. In a pottery class, there are no marks for perfect pots. Rather, such a class is an opportunity for you to let loose and allow your mind to be free and uninhibited. Other alternatives could be learning how to play an instrument or how to salsa dance. Once you take over the reins from the logical mind, you can allow your sixth sense to roam free because then the possibilities become endless.

Use All Senses Together

You don't want to become over-reliant on your sixth sense, as this could interfere with your decision-making processes and make you a tad bit paranoid. When overused, the sixth sense can be worn down. The important thing is to maintain a healthy balance between your third eye and all your other senses. This way, you filter your perception through different channels and arrive at the most informed conclusion.

Third Eye Chakra Cleansing

Chapter 5 introduces the concepts of chakras and their place in the empath's world. Feel free to go back to this chapter if you need some refreshing.

The third eye, otherwise known as the mind's eye or the sixth chakra, is thought to be an invisible eye that gives one a more heightened perception of things. In other words, the third eye is the well from which your sixth sense springs. In graphical illustrations, the third eye is usually shown to be located at the center of your forehead. When it comes to the third eye, there are three categories of empaths. The first category includes empaths who don't know of the third eye's existence, while the second category is made up of those who know it exists and use it sparingly, almost as if they are afraid of unleashing its full potential. The final category is made up of empaths who have embraced the full glory of the third eye and use its power and perception to direct their everyday decisions. Ideally, all empaths should open their third eye, which in this case means honing your sixth sense so that you can see what is beyond the ordinary.

There are many breathing and visualization exercises that are thought to unblock the third eye chakra. Engaging in such exercises prepares your third eye to be in an optimum state to detect and send out perceptions.

Here is a mini exercise:

1. First, you'll need to ensure that you are in a relaxed state, whether lying down or seated upright in a quiet room.

2. Slowly breath in and out deeply and repeat this ten times.

3. As you inhale and exhale, imagine a purple ball of light straight at the middle of your forehead where your

third eye is said to be located.

4. Imagine that the ball of light is collecting all the negative thoughts from your mind, with the intention of purging them. The more the ball of light grows, the more negative energy it purges.

5. Imagine yourself taking in the positive energy of your newly-cleansed third eye.

6. Repeat this exercise until you're certain that all the blockages of your third eye have been eliminated.

Be sure to do some further research into the third eye as it will provide great benefits for you. The reason why it's important to ensure the third eye is clear and working as designed is because if this isn't the case, an empath is likely to feel indecisive, overwhelmed, paranoid, hopeless, and maybe even insignificant and lacking in purpose. A fully functional third eye allows the empath to see beyond the minor details and focus on the bigger picture instead.

Embody Compassion in Your Everyday Life

Do not be so focused on honing your psychic abilities that you forget to live in your present and natural world where there are people that need your love and compassion. It might be exciting to live in a world that nobody else can see but you also run the risk of pushing away the people around you. Practice compassion in your everyday life and you will soon see some of it come back to you. When this happens, you will find yourself surrounded by positive energy, which will put you in an even better place to develop your abilities. Above all else, practice compassion for the simple reason that there are people who could really use it. The selfless compassion of a psychic empath is the never-ending well that nourishes others while feeding the empath as well.

Refuse to Tolerate Negative Energy

While practicing compassion in your daily life is a great act, it is important to realize that you will still come across negative people from time to time. If you grew up in a violent or negative household it is likely you have grown used to this sort of behavior and treatment. But this does not have to be your default anymore. You have a choice.

The old you may have tolerated and just 'dealt' with someone who likes to constantly complain and cause drama, or even worse, put you down, but the new empowered version of yourself must refuse to tolerate negative energy and negative people. Say 'no' and walk away. Respect yourself and love yourself.

Energy is contagious and therefore it is important to surround yourself with positive, uplifting, and inspiring energy. And by doing so, you will allow yourself to live a happier life and grow yourself and your abilities much higher providing greater internal fulfillment.

Build a Healthy and High Sense of Self-Worth

This is something that is not changed overnight but nonetheless a vital and healthy focus to have in order to become an empowered psychic empath warrior. There is no one particular step to increase your self-worth to a healthy and high level but rather a combination of many pieces of the puzzle. As you combine everything we have talked about so far, you unapologetically allow yourself to shine to the highest level and truly become a positive impact on the world providing massive value to people who also want to become better versions of themselves.

Chapter 7: Common Myths That Psychic Empaths Should Never Believe

As if being highly sensitive to the energy around you is not already a big responsibility, you will also have to contend with a lot of misconceptions about you. As an empath, you really have a big calling on your hands and you need to understand that not everyone will understand this. You might be labeled as being too emotional or too dramatic. You might even be accused of being one of the energy vampires that you are so keen to eliminate from your life. Understanding the many misconceptions that people have in regard to empaths is the first step towards gently educating those around you. Even if you do not feel like being the myth buster in your circle, you can still learn to differentiate the myths from the facts for your own sake. Knowledge is power and having knowledge about yourself is one of the most powerful things you can do for yourself.

Myth #1: Psychic empaths are extremely self-absorbed and only worry about themselves.

Fact: Psychic empaths often care about others more than they care about themselves.

From the outside looking in, the moodiness and emotional nature of a psychic empath can come across as the disposition of a person who is only concerned with how they are feeling. The truth of the matter is that a psychic empath is more likely to be moody because of the people around them, and not because of their own emotions. It is easy to be judgmental towards a psychic empath because of how they carry themselves. They are often quiet and reserved and will not want to come out to play too often. This might be interpreted to mean that they do not care about interacting with others and only worry about themselves. The truth is that while the empath might want to be a ray of sunshine to everyone else, they often find themselves incapable because of the overwhelming feelings they go through when dealing with different energies given out by others.

Myth #2: Psychic empaths are just mentally ill.

Fact: Being highly sensitive is not a mental illness.

Many empaths make for good listeners and confidants based on their ability to empathize and truly feel for others. Because of this, empaths often find themselves the designated dumping ground for all emotional baggage. When you are burdened with the emotional problems of others, it is easy to become depressed and anxious, which might cause others to assume you are mentally ill. Many times, empaths are just sad because of all the emotional burden that they have to shoulder. This immense sadness may mimic the signs of a person that is going through clinical depression. Yes, there are instances when an empath may be diagnosed with depression, but this is not simply because they are highly sensitive. There are numerous factors that must be present for one to be diagnosed with depression. These factors are not exclusive to an empath. They can affect just about anyone, especially those who are genetically predisposed to the same.

Myth #3: Empaths are psychologically weak

Fact: The moments of "weakness" that empaths exhibit are as a result of all the negative energy that they have to deal with.

What might be normal to a typical non-empath may be extremely difficult to the empath. Take, for instance, holding down an office job. For the person that is not highly sensitive to the energy of other people, an office job is just another opportunity to earn a paycheck and advance in their career. For the empath, an office job means being constantly bombarded by the negative energy from all sides. As such, an empath might struggle to hold down a normal 9 to 5 job, while this is just another workday for everyone else. When this happens, the empath might be accused of being weak, lazy, fussy or just unwilling to try. This could not be further from the truth. Being an empath is hard work. Imagine walking through life everyday while someone carries a huge ball that they hit you with every time you take one step. This is how it feels to be an empath. You are constantly being hit by a big ball of negative energy and you must lift yourself up every time you fall from this hit. After a while, it can be easier to stay on the ground because you have run out of energy to lift yourself up. As an empath, it is important to remember that you are not psychologically frail. Being able to deal with other people's negative energy on a daily basis and showing up in the world even though you know what's coming, takes a whole lot of strength.

Myth #4: Empaths are emotionally volatile

Fact: Being exposed to varying emotional energy can make you more in control of your emotions.

People who believe that empaths are emotionally volatile

base their arguments on the fact that empaths are often exposed to various energies, which might interfere with how emotionally stable they are. True, it is common for an empath to be moody, but this does not mean that they are always going to lash out when provoked. Many empaths are often moody when they retreat into themselves to introspect on the emotions that they have picked up. This does not make them a volatile person who is at the mercy of their emotions. It is possible for an empath to be highly stable when it comes to their feelings and those of others. In fact, an empath can easily learn how to be calm and in control regardless of those around them by understanding how to process and shield the energy that surrounds them. Some of the calmest and collected people that exist in this world are actually empaths. They have learned to read people and so nothing really takes them by surprise.

Myth #5: Most empaths are cold and detached from everyone else.

Fact: Detachment is a side effect of being emotionally drained.

As discussed in Chapter 3, it is possible for an empath to become detached over time if they have gone through tough periods of emotional drain. Many empaths who come across as detached do not become so because they intended to. It is often as a result of being emotionally abused by people around them. When they cannot take it anymore, an empath may become numb as a way of protecting themselves. It is not correct to assume that an empath is cold and unfeeling simply because they are an empath. Even the most outwardly detached empaths tend to have a light of empathy flickering deep inside of them. Empathy is not something you can switch on and off at will. If you care about other people, you will always care about them regardless of where you go or what you do.

Myth #6: Empaths are often highly dependent on their loved ones.

Fact: Empaths like for positive energy to flow both ways.

When an empath finds a source of positive energy, that source becomes an asset that they can draw their strength from. This is why empaths really thrive when they are deeply and genuinely loved. However, unlike energy vampires, empaths realize the need for the flow of positive energy to be two-sided. They love giving as much as they enjoy taking. You are not likely to find an empath that loves leeching on their loved ones. It is also important to note that empaths are not really dependent on positive energy from other people to survive. They are capable of doing it all on their own, as long as they learn how to protect from negative energy around them. If you are an empath, you do not have to worry about being a leech to others. As long as nobody is complaining, and as long as you can feel the good, positive energy flowing both ways, then it is safe to assume that the people in your life love you and the presence you bring.

Myth #7: Empaths are just glorified doormats.

Fact: With the right boundaries, an empath can care about others without feeling used.

Sure enough, empaths struggle with saying no. Empaths often want to take care of others and struggle with the guilt of feeling as if they are not helpful. It is effortless for an empath to find themselves relegated to the role of a doormat if they have not set the limits and boundaries for other people. This; however, does not mean that all sensitive people are just pushovers that allow anyone and everything in their lives. Empaths who are conscious of their powers and abilities know that it is easy for others to take advantage of them. As such, they often have ways of managing the people in their lives and striking the balance between being helpful and being everyone's doormat.

Myth #8: Empaths are all good people.

Fact: Being highly sensitive does not automatically qualify you for decency.

The question of whether a person is good or bad can only be answered after evaluating the choices that the person makes, and not as a factor of their genetic predisposition. Just because a person has been born as an empath does not mean they will always be a good person. An empath is a human being who is capable of hurting others and even making bad choices based on the prevailing circumstances in their life. While it is true that many empaths are often not manipulative people, it is also true that they are just humans and have the choice to be bad or good just like everyone else.

Myth #9: Empaths take to narcissists like moths to a light.

Fact: The relationship between empaths and narcissists is complex.

It has been said that opposites attract, and this could never be overstated in the case of narcissists and empaths. Empaths are the complete opposite of narcissists, and when these two categories of people meet there are often fireworks. Why is this so? Is it because the empath is keen on healing the narcissist? In many cases, the empath is not even aware that they are dealing with a narcissist. This might seem like a contradiction because after all, empaths are supposed to be intuitive and highly capable of reading other people's energy and intentions. Narcissism is a personality disorder that brings forth individuals who are highly manipulative. At the beginning of a relationship, the narcissist might make it seem as if they are the healer that the empath needs. As such, the empath will gravitate towards the narcissist because they seem kind and decent and loving. The narcissist, on the other hand, will pursue the empath because they love the adoration that the empath is able to give so freely. The narcissist-empath relationship evolves to become a highly toxic relationship where the empath keeps on giving and forgiving, while the narcissist cannot stop taking and creating chaos because that is what they thrive in. There is often never a happy ending when a narcissist and an empath meet and fall in love.

Myth #10: All empaths are introverted.

Fact: Empaths can be introverted, or not.

Empaths do not all come in one size. There are different sides to an empath. Some are introverted, some are extroverted, while some are ambiverts. In all fairness, the extroverted empath is rarer than the introverted empath. However, reliable sightings point to the existence of the paradox that is an empath who is extroverted. Being extroverted is more of a personality trait than anything else. As such, you can be a person that loves to be around people and at the same time be highly capable of tuning into the emotions of those people. An extroverted empath gets to live a very conflicting life in that they want to interact with people but at the same time, they do not want to be overwhelmed by it. This is unlike the case of the introverted empath who could not care much for crowds. If you are an extroverted empath, you will need to be careful about how much you take in from others before wearing yourself down. For every two or so hours spent in a crowd, make sure you take some time to catch your breath and process out the negative energy from your body.

Myth #11: You can quit being an empath.

Fact: Being an empath is a life-long sentence.

Many empaths would love to be able to wake up one day and find that their empathic abilities are all gone. It can be overwhelming to be the resident empath, and sometimes you will feel that you need a break from all the caring. Unfortunately, if you are born an empath there simply is no way out of it. Instead of fighting your power, the best thing you can do for yourself is to learn how to harness it for your own good, and for the good of those around you. For example, you can train yourself to learn how to distinguish your emotions from those of others so that you do not carry emotional loads that do not belong to you. You may not be able to stop being an empath, but you sure can learn how to carry this gift without breaking your back.

Myth #12: Empaths are victims of childhood trauma.

Fact: Trauma is not a prerequisite for empathy.

Some people believe that the only way a person can be as emotional as the empath typically is if that person has gone through some form of childhood trauma. It is wrong to assume that a person who is sensitive towards others and in regard to their own emotions is automatically coming from a place of great suffering. True, there are empaths who have suffered greatly at the hands of those who were supposed to love and protect them. However, it is inaccurate to think that the driving force behind empathy is trauma. Some people are simply born with the ability to be highly sensitive. What happens to them as they grow up is a whole different matter.

Conclusion

The life of a psychic empath is by no means easy, but the gift of psychic empathy is not a small one either. It has been said that great power comes with great responsibility. Such is the case of a psychic empath who has been gifted a rare ability to see into others. With this ability comes the need to ensure that the psychic empath remains fair to themselves while also impacting others positively with their gift. Psychic empaths struggle with this balance all their lives, especially because they are often dismissed as too emotional or too sensitive when they bring it up. This book is intended to ensure that you never have to conform to these labels because you will have known better by the time you get to the final chapter. With this book, you are now in a better position to articulate who you are and what you are capable of instead of simply worrying that you overreact to situations.

Hopefully, you have had your fair share of a-ha moments when reading this book while identifying the enemies in your life and understanding why you sometimes feel the way you do even though there seems to be no reasonable explanation for it. It is important to always keep in mind that as a psychic empath, your number one enemy is your mind and the things that you allow to go on in your mind. While energy vampires like narcissists and the like may attempt to suck the soul out of you, your mind is the real landmine. It is in your mind that you wallow in thoughts and emotions, overthinking and over-processing other people's feelings and moods. It is your mind that keeps you company when you retreat to the solitude of your alone time. It is your mind that can change whether you see your ability as a good thing or a thing that you wish you did not have.

Conquering your mind so that it works for you and not against you will be one of the bravest things that you do for yourself as a psychic empath. Chapter 4 and 5 are complete with practical suggestions of things that you can do to conquer your mind, one step at a time. These suggestions can be implemented on a short-term and long-term basis and have been grouped appropriately.

After conquering your mind, you will then be tasked with ensuring that you use your empathic abilities for good. This does not mean lying flat so that others can walk on you. It means that you will need to learn who can be helped and who will not benefit much from your concern. It's all a matter of balance.

Lastly, you must understand that you will have good days and bad days. As a psychic empath, there will be days when your mind will go on a thinking spree and emotions will overcome you. It is important to remember that before anything else, you are a human and you are allowed to experience the full extent of the human condition. You are allowed to have good days, bad days and everything in between. You are allowed to have days when you spend all your hours helping others, and the days when you lock yourself up in your house and binge-watch your favorite series. Just because you are a psychic empath does not mean that you are obliged to dedicate all your days to saving humanity. Save some for yourself. Be kind to yourself as you are to others. Enjoy the journey of exploring what adventures your gift will take you on. It is often in the most unexpected of moments that we stumble upon our true happiness. May you stumble upon your happiness as you heal yourself and others.

If you found this material anyway helpful and beneficial to you, please let me know in the form of a review. I would love to hear from you. It brings me great fulfillment to know that my work is able to help any of the lost souls out there.

Thank you.

Goodbye for now, psychic empath warrior.

Narcissism and Narcissistic Abuse Recovery

Free Yourself by Understanding the Narcissists Personality Disorder, What the Hell Happened in Your Relationship and How to Effectively Heal

Diana Ortega

Introduction

Love is a beautiful feeling that changes not only our demeanor but also how we see the world. Many times, relationships lift and transform us into better versions of ourselves. Unfortunately, relationships can also bring us down, if we end up putting our trust into the wrong type of people, those that live their whole life caring for one single thing: themselves. We call these people narcissists, and we'll learn later on how we can differentiate them from regular selfish people and what makes them so dangerous, not just as life partners but as "humans" in general.

Are we to blame for entrusting a narcissist with our hearts? No. Anyone, no matter how strong or smart, can fall into the trap of a narcissist. They are first-class manipulators that know how to get under your skin and make themselves detrimental to your survival. They know the game and how to play it, and they never stop playing it.

A relationship with a narcissist never works out well. No matter how hard you try to please or change them, you'll always be the "bad guy" and he or she the victim. Whatever you do will never be good enough, until your confidence melts away and you become a shadow of the person you once were. A relationship with a narcissist is one that you have to escape from and never look back on.

On a positive note, you are not alone. There have been people before you, that have fought and won. That managed to gain control of their lives and regain their happiness. People that are doing it now, alongside you, cutting ties with the most toxic people and starting their journey of healing. There will be people doing it in the future because as long as there are narcissists in our world, there will be victims.

No matter who you are, you can break free, and you can heal. It takes time, effort, a strong will, and hard work, but the pain will slowly diminish in intensity. Until all that's left of it is a life-changing experience, a new you and an awareness of 'red flag' people.

This book aims to help you understand what type of person you unknowingly let in your life, how they become like that, why you didn't see it from the very start, how they weaseled their way into your mind and caused damage that you might not even be aware of... But, most importantly, it aims to be a guide to rebuilding your life from the ground up and recovering from your traumatizing experience.

What is a Narcissist?

We all have people in our lives that are incredibly confident and think highly of themselves. But, while they might not be the most pleasant sort to have around, these people are at best egocentric, if they do manage to have a relatively normal life. Narcissists, on the other hand, have many problems in multiple areas of their life, such as work, relationships, and finances. So, what's the difference between a self-centered person and a narcissist? Why can one have a normal life while the other struggles?

First things first, narcissism is a personality disorder, that one is not born with but develops over time, in certain conditions. A person that has narcissistic personality disorder is described as having a visceral need for attention, an inflated sense of self-importance masking fragile self-esteem, and, perhaps the most notable of all, a complete lack of empathy for others. Empathy is the human trait that allows us to relate to other people's feelings and understand them. Without empathy, one is unable to build authentic human relationships. That is why a narcissist will never have healthy relationships, be it romantic or of other nature.

According to a study published in the *Journal of Clinical Psychiatry*, 7.7% of men, and 4.8% of women develop narcissistic personality disorder (NPD) in their lifetime. The study also determined that young adults, people that went through divorce or separation from their partner, and people of color had higher chances of becoming narcissists (Nordqvist, 2018). We can conclude that technically speaking; if the right conditions are met, anyone can become a narcissist, regardless of sex, race, or age; which comes as a contradiction to the popular belief that only males can be narcissists.

Now let's further focus on the traits of a narcissist, to understand the magnitude of this personality disorder fully, and at the end of this chapter, we'll see how it stands out from other well-known personality disorders such as psychopathy and sociopathy.

An exaggerated sense of self-importance

The self-importance that a narcissist experience is different from vanity or extreme confidence. It's best described as "grandiosity," which defines a sense of superiority built on unrealistic terms. Narcissists believe that they are unique and seek to associate themselves with people/places/situations of high status, as they perceive themselves as being too good for ordinary or average things. This sense of being better than others is often built inside their mind and not based on real-life achievements. They will expect others to treat them as if they are superior, and to do that; they will resort to lying about their abilities, achievements, and always paint themselves as being the better person in any situation, be it relationships or work-related.

In short, a narcissist plays the part of the superior one, in all aspects of life, and will resort to anything to maintain this status, including lying, twisting and diminishing others.

The constant need for attention and validation

While they do foster that sense of superiority, they are somewhat aware of the illusory aspect of it. This is why they need constant praise and recognition to keep the illusion alive. For a narcissist, compliments are not enough. They will seek people that will offer them constant validation, and that will cater to their needs at all times, without ever giving anything back. They expect the people around them to put them on a pedestal, and even the slightest of critiques will be taken as a personal attack and will result in the narcissist becoming abusive.

A relationship with a narcissist can only be one-sided. They are too self-absorbed and cannot put themselves in their partner's shoes and understand their feelings and emotions.

Entitlement

Despite them not being deserving of any special treatment, a narcissist will feel abnormally entitled to the finer things in life. They will expect people to act in a certain way and always be at their disposal. Anyone that does not comply with that will be met with some form of aggression, going as far as being cut from the narcissist's life. They believe that they deserve everything they wish for, and they are not afraid to show it.

Exploiting the people in their life

As we touched on briefly at the start of this chapter, narcissists are incapable of feeling empathy, almost like an empty vessel. For a narcissist, the people in their lives are only a means to an end, more like tools and objects than actual human beings. They do anything to satisfy their own needs, and they will resort to exploiting the people in their life, without feeling any remorse, guilt, or shame for it. This is why it is extremely dangerous to have a narcissist in your life. It is hard to truly understand how someone is incapable of feeling empathy, remorse, or guilt as these are all emotions most people experience, and we automatically assume all humans have.

Narcissists have no problem with exploiting anyone, in any situation, as long as they get what they want, and they will never take responsibility for hurting others. They will keep 'stonewalling' (avoiding answering questions, take responsibility for their actions as if you are speaking to a wall) you until you are confused and docile. All the relationships they build are based on their needs. They will often ensure that they have multiple people to cater to their needs, be it shelter, money, sex, or other sorts of favors.

Living in an imaginary world

A narcissist has a very frail relationship with reality. He or she prefers to live in their own fantasy world in which they can paint whatever image of themselves they want, pushing aside any details that don't work in their favor. They are willingly lying to themselves to protect the feeling of superiority that's detrimental to their survival, and annihilating contradictions or facts that go against their warped logic. Because they are insecure deep inside, this fantasy world works as their means of facing an unsatisfying reality. It allows them to feed their superiority with illusions of success, fame, popularity, and whatever they might need, and their defensive systems react heavily whenever something threatens or tries to reveal the illusion.

Putting others down to lift themselves up

The inner core of the narcissist is threatened by anyone that has something they lack, be it money, success, or simply the admiration of others. They will do anything to diminish a person that threatens their self-importance, by acting condescending, using insults, bullying, and any other means available to 'scoop out' someone's self-worth. No matter how much they end up hurting people, narcissists only care about keeping their own fantasies alive, and will never feel remorseful or take responsibility for their actions.

Monopolizing

A conversation with a narcissist is pretty much like watching TV. They like to be the center of attention, and they will do whatever they can to have the last word, even if that means cutting others short or acting as if others have nothing valuable to say. Everything must revolve around them, no matter what, and they will display strong feelings of envy whenever they are not the focal point of a situation.

With a narcissist, everything is one-sided: relationships, conversations, situations. Simply because they are solely interested in themselves, and anything else only matters if they can use it to their own benefit.

Unstable mood

Whenever they find themselves slipping from their fantasy and face how far from the perfect persona they actually are, a narcissist will display a wide range of emotions. They will feel vulnerable, sad, and might even experience episodes of depression. Also, because of their weak ability to cope with reality, they have a tough time adapting to change or new situations, and they handle stress poorly. In the last effort to protect themselves, narcissists will lash out to the people around them, abusing them to regain that sense of superiority and control that they need. They won't back down from anything if it means that their illusion is kept alive. This fragility combined with their lack of empathy, remorse, and guilt makes the narcissist a toxic, abusive factor in any relationship, no matter how hard the other person may try to please them.

There is a great deal of confusion regarding three well-known types of personality disorders, that being narcissism, psychopathy, and sociopathy. What sets them apart from each other? How do we know what we are dealing with?

Both psychopathy and sociopathy are considered special types of personality disorders called antisocial personality disorders. They share multiple traits such as deceitfulness, aggression, irritability, a tendency towards committing criminal acts, lack of remorse or empathy in general, and not being able to take responsibility for their actions.

What sets them apart from the very beginning is that psychopaths are born while sociopaths are made. What does that mean? It is widely agreed that, although environmental factors, traumas, and different types of abuse influence both disorders, psychopathy is the main result of a faulty development in the parts of the brain that deal with emotions and impulse control. Psychopaths lack emotions and an ability to comprehend emotional responses from early infancy while sociopaths are results of trauma, and they can develop this disorder in any stage of their life. The rates of sociopathy are quite high. Statistically, 1 in 25 US citizens is a sociopath, which is very grim.

Narcissists share some traits with these antisocial disorders such as the lack of empathy and their inflated sense of self, but they are usually not aggressive in a physical way, and they are not impulsive. A narcissist's aggression comes from their verbal abuse and manipulation and is rarely physical. Their need to be admired by others, and thus their dependence on other people's attention also sets them apart from the field of antisocial personality disorders. Out of the two, we could say that narcissism most resembles sociopathy, seeing as it is a disorder that comes as a result of multiple factors and is not caused by undeveloped brain functions. It's only the narcissist's desire to achieve "perfection" that makes him less likely to commit criminal acts, that distinctively sets them apart from the destructive sociopath.

Knowing what a narcissist is, and what it's not, is crucial if you want to understand the sort of person that you have or had next to you, and how to successfully break free from them. Don't forget that, their lack of empathy makes it impossible to have a healthy relationship with them, so it's not your fault that it didn't work out. You deserve to be happy and loved, as much as anyone else in this world, so never feel guilty about leaving a narcissist behind.

A Relationship with a Narcissist

Any sort of relationship with a narcissist brings upon challenges, especially if we are talking about a romantic one. What they look for in a partner is a supply, not an equal. And in their quest of satisfying their own needs, they will end up destroying you, both mentally and emotionally. That's because, at the end of the day, the more broken and vulnerable you are, the more likely you're to remain in that relationship, a prisoner to a cruel and unsympathetic torturer that takes pleasure in your misery.

The best way to describe what effect a relationship with a narcissist will have on you is by using a popular analogy. Have you heard of the frog and the pot of water analogy? If a frog jumps into a pot of boiling water, it will immediately jump out, because it will perceive it as painful and dangerous. The sudden increase in temperature is easily recognizable for the frog. But what if our frog jumps into the water before we put it on the stove? It will feel rather pleasant to stay in room temperature water, right? What if, then we start to gradually heat the water until it reaches its boiling point? What happens to the frog? Unfortunately, it will remain in the water until its untimely death, because it is much harder for the frog to perceive the gradual slight increase in temperature. In other words, you wouldn't jump into a relationship with a person that is obviously selfish, emotionless, and self-centered, but you would stay in a relationship that starts off exciting and romantic but gradually withers away over time. And you would do it out of love. However, just like our frog, a part of you will die along with the relationship, as the boiling waters of narcissism will melt away your confidence, self-worth, and love for yourself.

Another way to look at a narcissistic relationship is to compare it with the old Chinese torture and execution method known as "death by a thousand cuts." In this practice, a knife is used to slowly and methodically cut away portions of someone's body, over a prolonged period of time, until the victim finally succumbs to its fate. It's cruel, atrocious, and unfortunately, the best way to describe narcissistic abuse. A narcissist will slowly cut away pieces of the image you have of yourself, until your whole identity "dies," leaving behind just a doll that the narcissist can move and play with as they please. This is because of their deep insecurities mixed with their desire to control you.

Now let's take it back a notch and understand how a relationship with a narcissist develops, and what are some tell-tale signs that you are in a relationship with a person that has NPD.

You must understand that a narcissist knows how to act in order to make themselves desirable. They are charming and captivating, drawing you in with their boisterous display of personality. They have a cunning capacity for "reading people" and finding out exactly what they want from a romantic partner. Once they have you "figured out," they will perfectly emulate your ideal man/woman until they get you to fall in love with them. These stages of pre-relationship and early relationship are the pinnacle of your love story. These moments will bring you genuine happiness, bliss, and the sense that you have found your soulmate. You will feel like you are in your own romance book/movie, and everything will seem perfect. The narcissist will shower you with compliments, gifts, their undivided attention, and they will cater to your needs. Perhaps this sounds all familiar to you. But, once they are confident that you have fallen in love with them, they will begin to change. Gradually, the water will start heating up, while you bathe in the pot, unaware of the impending danger.

The exciting honeymoon period will abruptly stop as the narcissist starts to display self-centered behaviors. As Dr. W. Keith Campbell, an expert in NPD, explains, "The effects of narcissism are most substantial in relation to interpersonal functioning. In general, trait narcissism is associated with behaving in such a way that one is perceived as more likable in initial encounters with strangers— but this likability diminishes with time and increased exposure to the narcissistic individual." Once the magical dust clears off, it will already be too late for the partner. At this point, they will start playing their manipulative games, exploiting you and your trust for their own needs. Transforming a love story into a one-sided play in which you will feel lonelier than ever, as the narcissist starts controlling your life and pushing your family and friends away.

The abuse is subtle (ambient abuse) but deadly as they start off by making you feel special and amazing, following by a malicious spur of words and actions meant to devalue you as a person and bring you down. You will always be the one at fault, the inferior one. Your achievements will be diminished or ignored. Your entire existence will seem more of an annoyance to the narcissist, and, once you start denying him or her the recognition or satisfaction they demand, they will discard you. It could be a gradual process, where they start planting the seed of the break-up with remarks and cheating sprees, or it could be abrupt and without reason. Either way, a relationship with a narcissist almost never ends there. They will keep tabs on you and try to get back in your life whenever they are in need of immediate gratification, only to discard you again afterward. This will happen as many times as you allow it to, which is why it is so difficult to escape narcissistic abuse. Especially after they have already brought you to the most vulnerable point in your life, the amount of power and effort to refuse them is enormous. You will *want* to forgive them and give them a second chance. NPD sufferers know how to target their victims, and they mostly choose compassionate people with over-the-top kindness.

Early signs that your partner might be a narcissist:

1. He/she interrupts you when you speak.

2. He/she has a habit of breaking the rules or violating social norms (for example, they might cut in line, treat waiters poorly, often disobey traffic laws and so on).

3. They are always overly attentive with their appearance and take pleasure in making others jealous.

4. Inability to apologize or will feign it and not truly mean it.

5. Inability to take responsibility for their actions. Will resort to 'playing the victim' in arguments and moments of conflict. Nothing is ever their fault.

6. Speaking about themselves in very high terms and comparing themselves to heroes/celebrities/successful people.

7. Having high expectations for you to satisfy their needs.

8. Has the habit of borrowing things or money without returning them.

9. Might push you to overstep personal boundaries.

10. He/she has a very hot and cold personality in your relationship; being overly affectionate/flattering

whenever he/she needs something from you and ignoring you when you fail to meet their needs/try to hold them responsible for their actions/words.

11. He/she overreacts because he/she can't distinguish between small events and important issues. The smallest things can lead to a bombastic reaction.

12. He/she is always right, no matter what. Their views and opinions are the only ones that matter to them.

13. He/she expects you to do whatever they ask you to, without questioning them or hesitating.

14. They use threats a lot, most of them falling either into "I'll break up with you" category or "I will ruin your reputation" category.

15. They make you feel guilty about your actions/decisions, often in situations where there is nothing to feel guilty of.

To recap, relationships with narcissists start on very good terms, as they trick you into believing that you have found the one. This is when they have their "mask" on. The first few weeks/months will be amazing, exciting, passionate, and it will make you deeply love and care for them. By the time they start showing their true colors and "letting the mask slip", it's too late to avoid the abuse that follows. Your brain will refuse to accept the new reality. You will cling and hold on dearly to the initial person you met and the amazing emotions you felt in the beginning.

They will begin using you as their supplier for love, admiration, monetary needs, and whatever desires they will have. Any refusal or critique to the narcissist will be taken as a personal attack (narcissistic injury) and will prompt a bombastic reaction, that will fizzle out as quickly as it started. On an emotional level, the relationship is completely one-sided, you being the only one that loves and cares for him/her.

If you believe that you might be in a narcissistic relationship and you want to break the cycle of abuse, your only option is cutting them from your life, no matter how hard that might be. Later on, in this book, we will talk about advice and strategies to escape from an abusive relationship.

If you already managed to get free of the narcissist's influence, but you have no idea how to regain control over your own life and heal from the abuse, hang tight. We will discuss this later in the book, so don't lose hope. The healing process might be long, and it will take a lot of effort, but in the end, you will get back your happiness and leave this part of your life behind.

In any situation you might be, one thing will never change: relationships with narcissists aren't healthy, and they will destroy you, especially on an emotional level. They are manipulators and abusers by nature, and it's very hard for a person that suffers from NPD to change. Therapy may or may not help them regain some of that humanity they lost, but they first have to acknowledge the fact that they need help. That they are not fine. Since that recognition would put a big hole in their illusion of grandiosity, it doesn't happen that much, and when it does, it's on their own accord. "Fixing them" is not something you can do.

Your only options are: staying in that abusive relationship or escaping from it and taking back control over your life. And only one of them will truly make you happy.

The Birth of a Narcissist

Narcissism usually has roots in early childhood, but it often starts manifesting in a person's teen years and early adulthood. It is widely believed that children who have been victims of abuse, neglect, or otherwise faulty parenting will grow up to display narcissistic behavior, while research is still carried on regarding a possible genetic predisposition to developing NPD. Recent evidence shows that biochemical factors are also to be taken into consideration regarding the origin of narcissism. Highly sensitive people also have a somewhat higher risk of developing NPD as an unhealthy coping mechanism.

Let's start with childhood. Being selfish is part of an infant's development, as it ensures that their immediate needs, such as hunger, are being met. A young child does not have the capacity to understand someone else's feelings or needs, so its focus stays on their own existence. For the child to develop properly and become a functional member of society, this selfishness needs to decline gradually. The child needs to learn how to see life from someone else's perspective and start paying attention to the needs and feelings of others - the basis of empathy. If there is no emotional development, or if the child grows up believing that being vulnerable is not acceptable, then it automatically has a higher risk of being a narcissist in the future. However, clinicians believe that NPD can't be, and shouldn't be diagnosed in children, as it would be incongruent.

Parenting styles that could lead to the creation of a narcissist include: neglecting, setting very high expectations for them, cold/insensitive, overly indulgent, promoting an entitled attitude, and overly controlling.

Trauma and abuse are also two factors that can't be ignored, as they are influential psychological factors. Children, pre-teens, and teens that go through traumatic events or any abuse will have a higher risk of developing bad coping mechanisms or planting the seeds for narcissism, compared to young adults or adults. Even death in the family can be the start of a warped way of dealing with reality if the child doesn't have a positive example to follow or someone to guide him/her through it. Remember that for narcissism, the origins are usually in early childhood, although it can be clinically diagnosed only after the age of 18.

Teenagers, for example, tend to be self-centered, as they are in a confusing time of their lives where they feel the need to be independent. So, it's harder to tell if they are displaying potential narcissistic tendencies or if they are just being rebellious. But there are some red flags that one could notice, even in this early stage of creation of a possible narcissist, such as:

- Overly competitive, to the point that the teen does not mind hurting others as long as he/she wins.

- Lying to get their way/lying whenever it is beneficial for them to lie - without taking responsibility for it.

- Never taking responsibility for their actions/words and blaming others.

- Egotistical to the point where they only care about their themselves and getting their needs catered to, above anyone else's.

- A sense of entitlement that has no real basis other than the fact that they believe they should be treated specially.

- Having bully tendencies to the extent of becoming verbally abusive/diminishing people with their words.

- Overreacting to criticism, even when it is constructive.

So, after the seed is planted, and we have a mind that doesn't know how to process emotions or how to understand people, what happens? How is a narcissistic mind built? How does it process the world?

After a traumatic event happens in early childhood, the child develops negative feelings, such as shame, towards their "real self." To combat that, this "real self" is buried deep down, and the child suffers from arrested development of their emotional intelligence, keeping emotions such as love, compassion, or their full capacity to feel empathy, severely underdeveloped. Besides relinquishing this "real self" and in order to cope, the child creates a "false self," a mask created by mimicking other people's way of acting that the child finds admirable.

This "split personality" of theirs makes it very hard to spot the narcissist. They can publicly act like regular members of society while in private they abuse and mistreat anyone close to them. Protecting their real self by nurturing and maintaining their false self is the fundament and basis of the narcissist's behavior. To achieve that, a narcissist needs constant reassurance and admiration, which are also called "narcissistic supplies." They depend on these supplies and will do anything to get them, by using manipulation tactics, lies, and abuse. Any critique will remind them of the real self they are hiding, causing hostile defensive responses.

The real self has the following characteristics:

- Buried deep inside their psyche.

- Bears feelings of extreme self-loathing, shame, misery, jealousy of "normal people."

- Desperate protection from being exposed to the world.

- Abusing the people closest to them, the narcissist escapes momentarily from having to deal with their real self.

- Completely passive/paralyzed, has no active role in the conscious mind of the narcissist - making psychotherapy treatment very challenging.

The false self is characterized as:

- A mask/camouflage to hide the real self.

- A shield for the real self.

- Confident, charming, charismatic.

- Rude/impolite to those that he/she believes to be beneath them.

- Prone to explosions of anger - narcissistic fury, and hostility if critiqued - although they pass as fast as they come; when the narcissist feels threatened, we say that he/she suffers a "narcissistic injury."

- Manipulative - knows exactly how to get the attention of a wide variety of people.

- Having a wide circle of people, they know, but no deep relationships - everything is superficial.

- Pathological liar.

Between these two sides of the same coin, there is no competition regarding "who takes control." The real self depends on the false self to survive and cope with reality. Without the presence of the false self, the true self is in danger of disappearing and "dying." By developing this false self, a child becomes immune to the abuse/trauma that it's been through. It shields the true self from pain, and negative emotions, while also actively "hiding" it from the outside world. For the narcissist, their only "self" is the "false self," as it allows him/her to be a "better" version of themselves, one that deserves to be treated better. Although, in essence, this false self starts as a reaction to the abuse/trauma, or a way to adapt to an unhappy life, it ends up being the predominant "self," suffocating the true self and making emotional and personal growth impossible.

The fact that there is a true self, which is weak, underdeveloped, and crippled, and a false self which dominates the psyche of the narcissist, is pretty straightforward and easy to understand. What's harder to pinpoint is how connected these two halves are? Exactly what behaviors can be attributed to which and are there interchangeable? Can the false self "borrow" from the true self's personality in order to fool the world?

The reality is that there are different degrees of "narcissism." A spectrum that goes from milder cases to extremely severe ones. Some narcissists might still show, from time to time, glimpses of his/her true self, meaning that it is not completely passive. However, these cases are fairly rare, and most narcissists simply create a false self that imitates their true selves. Nevertheless, we can go further and settle on two main types of narcissists: The grandiose narcissist and the vulnerable narcissist. These two types originate from different types of childhood experiences, and they manifest in contradictory ways.

The grandiose narcissists are the result of growing up as an entitled kid, who was overly spoiled and was led to believe that he or she was superior and better than the other kids. This type of narcissist tends to be more dominant, aggressive, and very open to telling people how great they are. In relationships, grandiose narcissists are prone to cheating and abruptly leaving their partners when their needs are no longer satisfied.

The vulnerable narcissists are more aware of the illusory aspect of their grandiosity, and they have frequent mood swings. This type of narcissism is usually the result of trauma or neglect, and they feel victimized or attacked whenever things don't go their way. Although they are more sensitive than the grandiose narcissists, they still lack any sort of empathy, and they become dependent on their partners to offer constant supplies to feed their illusions. In a relationship, the vulnerable narcissist will often doubt the sincerity and faithfulness of their partners, while also showing increasing levels of possessiveness and jealousy.

Regardless of the exact type of narcissist, you're dealing with, they all function on the same "true self - false self" system.

How does the false self work? The narcissist employs two mechanisms: re-interpretation and emulation. Re-interpretation is the act of taking emotions and reactions in a positive light. To be more precise, any emotion or reaction that the narcissist does not consider to be socially acceptable or good are warped into something else. Fear, for example, turns into compassion, because that is a feeling that will earn him/her admiration while fear is considered humiliating. By re-interpreting, the narcissist keeps its false self thriving, feeding the illusion of moral superiority.

Emulation is completely different, although the purpose it serves is ultimately the same. While narcissists do not feel or understand empathy, they excel when it comes to simulating emotions. They are first-class observers of human behavior, and they know exactly how to act in certain situations, in order to give the illusion of empathy. This is used to get under their victim's skin and annihilate their natural defenses. They have the ability to get in someone's mind, and they use it to fulfill their need for control and reassurance. In other words, by emulating emotions and empathy, they hook their victims, ensuring a constant supply of whatever they desire, be it admiration, praise, monetary gains, or other types of favors.

Whether we like to admit it or not, narcissists were originally victims, that, in the absence of any guidance and help, built up their own way of dealing with things. One that ended up being toxic for everyone, including the narcissist. Narcissists should be pitied as much as feared because, at the end of the day, they will never know true happiness. Their life is a drama show, created to fool others. They depend on the admiration of their audience. That being said, that doesn't make the narcissist a humanitarian because you should not take it upon yourself to fix him or her. Even specialists have a hard time helping them, and that would also require the narcissist to admit that he or she needs help - which does not happen often. After heavily depending on the false-mask for so long, it is extremely difficult for the narcissist to work towards killing the false-self and developing the real self.

No matter how hard it might be to accept, the narcissist only sees you as supply, an object to be used, and nothing more, and while you are still offering up what he/she needs, the abuse will never stop. Being abusive is their second nature. They can't help it, but you can put an end to it. Leaving an abuser is the first step towards a better life. Your happiness matters!

Unfortunately, a particular group of people with loving and admirable traits get sucked into the narcissist's reality. When these types of people fall in love with a narcissist, it is usually a very long, painful nightmare. Accepting the reality that the narcissist cannot be fixed is challenging, and in most cases, a reality where the victim's beautiful qualities and self-worth are scooped out over time. I know this sounds daunting and depressing right now but have hope. There is light at the end of the tunnel.

In the next chapter, we will look into what exactly these qualities are that narcissists are attracted to when looking for their next victim.

How Narcissists Choose Their Victims

When faced with a skillful emotional predator, most of us would be vulnerable, simply because we are humans. However, narcissists, much like other types of predators, have their preferences. Some traits will make you more likely to be the victim of a narcissist. That being said, it does not mean that the personality traits we are about to go through, are bad or somewhat wrong. In the context of a healthy relationship, these traits would provide the perfect basis for positive developments and growth for both partners. There is no need for you to feel bad about having these traits. But you do have to be wary of the type of people that will be drawn to you, and how they use these traits against you for their own advantage, so you can protect yourself in the future.

Let's see what a narcissist looks for in a person. Maybe this will answer the inevitable question that you probably asked yourself a million times before: "Why me?"

Empathy

The trait that narcissists love the most in their victims. Empathy mixed with deep emotions of love makes for an easy target to manipulate from the narcissist's perspective. Although narcissists themselves are not capable of being empathetic, it is crucial for their survival to target people that have a great deal of empathy. An empathic partner gives the narcissist the emotional fuel it needs to keep his or her false perception of themselves alive. An empathic person will offer everything in a relationship and will always try to see the situation from the other's perspective, something that facilitates the narcissistic abuse cycle.

This otherwise empowering ability to understand other people's feelings turns into a double-edged sword in the hands of a narcissist. They know that, with such a person, playing victim is a breeze. They will always have an audience for their self-directed and written "drama." They know that they will be forgiven, no matter how much their words/actions have hurt you, and thus, they will never have to take any responsibility.

An empathic person will also hesitate to hold their partners accountable or expose their bad behavior to the world. They feel somewhat compelled to protect their abusers and forgive them, out of a strong sense of guilt. Narcissists know that an empathic person will always put their needs first, making them easy to use tools in their quest of getting what they want/believe they deserve. Also, the forgiving nature of an empathic person makes them more likely to return to an abusive relationship. Empaths are generally kind-hearted individuals that are focused on making the people in their life happy, so we can say they are often "people pleasers." But something else that the narcissist can benefit from is the empath's inability to draw a line. They often have weak boundaries, out of love for their partner and out of a lack of self-worth, which is why they constantly accept/do things they might not be comfortable with.

Long story short: high empathy equals high chances of becoming the target of a narcissist.

This is why we see a lot of Narcissists dating Empaths. You may even be an Empath.

Perfectionism

It may sound weird, but narcissists like to go for people that are extreme perfectionists. These types of people are never satisfied with what they do/achieve, and they genuinely believe there is always room for improvement. A narcissist knows how to use this personality trait in his/her favor. It's a lot easier to convince a perfectionist, that always seeks to please others and that's forever doubtful of everything they do, that they are not good enough. Narcissists will use this insecurity and desire of acknowledgment as a weapon against their partner, especially in the devaluation stage of the relationship.

A perfectionist will always diminish their worth and the importance/quality of their work. For a narcissist, that's extremely convenient.

Conscientiousness

A conscientious person always thinks about what's best for the people around them, and they have the habit of keeping their promises and taking responsibility for their actions. Unfortunately, such people also tend to make the mistake of projecting their idea of morality on others, which will leave them under the false impression that the narcissist will do the same.

A narcissist knows that a conscientious person is one that can be exploited, as they are very likely to offer second chances, will be generally forgiving, and will have a hard time believing that their romantic partner is not as good of a person as they initially thought. Conscientious people also know that in order for a relationship to work, both members have responsibilities and obligations, and often, they will give way and compromise their own happiness in order to please their partners.

Dr. George Simon, an author that's very interested in the ins and outs of narcissistic manipulation, sheds more light onto why conscientiousness is one of the most crucial traits that attract narcissists:

"Disturbed characters most often target folks possessing two qualities they don't possess: *conscientiousness* and *excessive agreeableness* (i.e. deference). So, it's a solid conscience that makes you most vulnerable to narcissistic manipulation. Manipulators use guilt and shame as their prime weapons. But you have to have the capacity for shame and guilt for the tactics to work. Disturbed characters lack that capacity. Conscientious folks have it in spades.

A narcissist might complain about how unfair you are. And because you inherently want to be fair, you take the complaint seriously. It might not occur to you that guilting or shaming you in this way is a tactic. You realize it later when they've taken advantage too many times.

Always having to be "right" pretty much defines narcissistic pride. Conscientious people care about right and wrong. And they don't like being in the wrong. So, all the narcissist has to do is to point out legitimate weaknesses, shortcomings, inconsistencies, minor errors, or missteps. Before you know it, you start seeing things their way. And worse, once you do, you're at greater risk to *defer*."

Intelligence

Narcissists look for people with an above-average intelligence, which are highly skilled and passionate about their careers. Why? Because, in the initial phase of the relationship, the partner is used as an "accessory" to add up to the narcissist's sense of superiority. They take pride in showing their partners off and being associated with them, as long as they remain the main focus of attention.

It may seem contra-productive for a narcissist to go for someone that will sooner or later threaten their sense of superiority, but the truth is that they take pleasure in putting down bright, passionate individuals. In a way, they get to share your spotlight while it lasts and then slowly take away all of your confidence and self-worth, which is a two-in-one package for narcissists.

Integrity

Individuals with integrity are very attractive to narcissists as they offer a lot of opportunities for exploitation. A person with integrity will most likely feel strongly against breaking off a relationship that they have invested in, even if the said relationship is not a positive one. They are open to forgiving their partners, and they don't like to get confrontational. They are very aware of the obligations that a relationship entrails, and they will compromise and try to alleviate conflicts, even if that means giving in.

A narcissist takes all these positive aspects of having integrity and turns them into ways of exploiting and chipping away at the self-trust of their partners. Their strong sense of morality becomes the shackles that keep the abusive relationship going until the narcissist puts an end to it.

Low Self-Esteem and Confidence

Insecurities are part of being human, and narcissists themselves are incredibly fragile when it comes to their perception of themselves. They fight to the death to protect their inflated sense of self. It comes as a logical choice for them to go after people who have self-esteem and confidence issues. Firstly, because they will respond very well to the initial phase of the relationship in which the narcissist "love bombs" its victim. People with insecurities crave compliments and acknowledgment, and the narcissist is more than prepared to deliver.

Secondly, a person that already has issues with how they perceive themselves will be much easier to take apart once the idealization is over. Narcissists have this malicious pleasure to diminish others. The more ammunition they have to accomplish that, the better. In a relationship with a narcissist, your insecurities will always be used against you.

Sentimentality

A sentimental person that's prone to romanticizing a relationship is, perhaps, one of the narcissist's favorite targets. Don't forget that narcissists dedicate the beginning of the relationship to making you feel special and catering to your needs. By doing that, they give a sentimental person, nice memories to cherish and feed on when they start showing their true colors.

Narcissists enjoy games, and they excel at playing with their partner's emotions. They know exactly what they need to say or do, to fabricate that "soulmate" feeling that will make their victims addicted to them, in a deep emotional way. Sentimental people are easy to pick up because they already have that native desire for meaningful human connection - something that a narcissist can mimic effortlessly.

Dr. Paul Babiak and Dr. Robert Hare talk about the way in which a predator assesses their victim and how they are able to fake a genuine bond. Although their book, *"Snakes in Suits: When Psychopaths Go to Work,"* focuses on psychopathic individuals, the next excerpt, from the chapter *Forging the Psychopathic Bond*, offers a very good understanding on how a sentimental person can be manipulated by emotional predators:

"As interaction with you proceeds, the psychopath carefully assesses your persona. Your persona gives the psychopath a picture of the traits and characteristics you value in yourself. Your persona may also reveal, to an astute observer, insecurities or weaknesses you wish to minimize or hide from view. As an ardent student of human behavior, the psychopath will then gently test the inner strengths and needs that are part of your private self and eventually build a personal relationship with you by communicating (through words and deeds) four important messages.

The first message is that the psychopath likes and values the strengths and talents presented by your persona. In other words, the psychopath positively reinforces your self-presentation, saying, in effect, I like who you are. Reinforcing someone's persona is a simple, yet powerful, influence technique, especially if communicated in a convincing—that is, charming—manner. Unfortunately, many people we deal with in our personal and professional lives are so self-absorbed and narcissistic that they rarely see our persona because of the preoccupation they have with their own. Finding someone who pays attention to us, who appreciates or actually "sees" us, is refreshing; it validates who we are and makes us feel special."

Resilience

Being able to bounce back from adverse situations is generally an incredible strength to possess. Unfortunately, narcissists also like having partners that can sustain a lot of "emotional damage" without leaving them. Survivors of abuse or different types of traumas are known to try hard to make everything right, and narcissists get a lot of benefits by being into a relationship with these types of people.

Their "savior syndrome" makes them fight for the relationship and try to "heal" their narcissistic partner, even if, deep inside they know that it's in vain. They get attached to toxic individuals and, what's worse is that they may even equal the amount of abuse they are put through with how much the other person must love them.

A narcissist will almost have an unlimited source of "narcissistic supplies" from a resilient person, as, no matter the amount of pain and abuse, they are very likely to stick around and jump immediately back into the relationship whenever the narcissist hoovers them.

A resilient person that has already been through trauma and abuse is also more prone to getting hooked on small gestures of affection, becoming effectively addicted to the other person. Dr. Joseph Carver, a clinical psychologist, explains in more detail how sporadic acts of kindness can trick resilient people into falling victims of the narcissist's abuse. Dr. Carver focuses on how that manipulation method is used by abusers to "trick" victims of Stockholm Syndrome, but the information is still relevant regardless of the type of abuse the victim has sustained.

"When an abuser/controller shows the victim some small kindness, even though it is to the abusers benefit as well, the victim interprets that small kindness as a positive trait of the captor... Abusers and controllers are often given positive credit for not abusing their partner, when the partner would have normally been subjected to verbal or physical abuse in a certain situation... Sympathy may develop toward the abuser, and we often hear the victim of Stockholm Syndrome defending their abuser with 'I know he fractured my jaw and ribs... but he's troubled. He had a rough childhood!'

Similar to the small kindness perception is the perception of a 'soft side.' During the relationship, the abuser/controller may share information about their past – how they were mistreated, abused, neglected, or wronged. The victim begins to feel the abuser/controller may be capable of fixing their behavior or worse yet, that they (abuser) may also be a 'victim.'

The admission is a way of denying responsibility for the abuse. While it may be true that the abuser/controller had a difficult upbringing – showing sympathy for his/her history produces no change in their behavior and in fact, prolongs the length of time you will be abused. While 'sad stories' are always included in their apologies–after the abusive/controlling event–their behavior never changes! Keep in mind; once you become hardened to the 'sad stories,' they will simply try another approach."

According to Dr. Carver, manipulators and abusers have learned to shift the blame on a variety of factors from being influenced by violent video games to the extreme of pinpointing "eating too much" as a valid reason for committing murder. They will invent any story if it benefits their exoneration of "bad deeds." Never trust an abuser's excuses no matter how reasonable they may sound.

Codependency

Leaving these traits aside for a bit, you should also know that people with codependent tendencies are too on the narcissist's "wishlist." Codependency is an emotional and behavioral condition which drastically affects a person's ability to have and maintain a normal, healthy relationship. This type of person always finds themselves in one-sided relationships which are abusive or destructive in nature. A codependent person develops what's known as "relationship addiction" that makes it very hard for them to escape from a toxic partner.

Traditionally, codependency was used to describe relationships with people that struggled with an alcohol or drug addiction. Then the term widened its area of use, after observed similarities of behavior, to also describe relationships with people that have some type of mental illness.

The roots of codependency are established in early childhood. Kids that are part of dysfunctional families are very likely to grow up with codependent tendencies. A dysfunctional family is one in which members suffer from negative emotions (anger, fear, pain, or shame) as a result of a problem that is widely ignored/denied by the said members. What are the most frequent problems hidden under the rug, by members of dysfunctional families? For starters, the existence of abuse, in any shape or form, be it physical, emotional, or even sexual. Then there is the existence of one member who battles some sort of addiction - be it substance abuse or gambling, a toxic relationship, etc. And last but not least, the existence of a family member that suffers from a chronic physical or mental illness.

Because these problems are ignored, family members develop the behavior of repressing their feelings and starting to put the needs of others above their own. That's how most of the resilient people that I have talked about before are born, the so-called "survivors." They learn ways to go around negative emotions, and they fully dedicate themselves to taking care of the person that struggles with addiction/illness, often sacrificing their own needs. These sorts of people can quickly lose sight of what they want and need, overall being prone to struggling with their own identity and sense of self.

Codependent people are characterized by low self-esteem, to the point in which they need something or someone from the outside to latch onto, in order to feel good about themselves. This type of behavior usually ends with some kind of addiction or with the development of compulsive behaviors (like workaholism). In a relationship, a codependent individual has the best intentions but, unknowingly takes on the role of the caretaker, seeking to satisfy the other person's needs. Besides taking care of their partners, they also protect them from having their bad behaviors known to the world and will often make excuses for the way they act in certain situations that may be condemned by others. As the relationship unfolds, the codependent person starts getting a feeling of reward and satisfaction from the fact that they are needed by someone. At some point, they start realizing that they have nothing to say regarding the way the relationship is going but they can't break away from the abuse, addicted to the feeling of validation that the partners give them.

Some characteristics of codependent people include: a sense of responsibility for the actions of others, addiction to relationships in need of validation and to avoid feeling abandoned, lack of trust in their own capabilities, problems with maintaining boundaries, difficulties when it comes to making decisions, a tendency of trying to "save" and "heal" people they are in a relationship with, easily hurt when no one acknowledges their work/effort, and a clear tendency to do more than they need, in any situation.

If you are/were in a relationship with a narcissist/abusive partner, and you were in any way "addicted" to being with that person, that does not automatically make you a codependent individual. You may only have a tendency towards putting your partner's needs above your own and doing your best to keep the relationship alive, despite constant problems. Remember that the narcissist is a first-class manipulator, that knows how to play his/her cards in order to get you hooked and secured. Understand that a victim of narcissistic abuse is very vulnerable and would rather cling to the failed relationship, out of hope for better days, than go back into the dating world. The trust and self-esteem of a victim of narcissistic abuse and their whole image of themselves have been damaged so severely that the simple thought of going back into their lives alone, without a partner to occasionally validate them, is too much to handle. However, if you do believe that you fit the profile of codependency, there are ways to improve your situation, by going to therapy and learn to experience all the emotions repressed due to childhood abuse or having a dysfunctional family.

Empaths

I mentioned this term earlier in the empathy section, and since we're talking about a narcissist's perfect victim, we can't oversee empaths. An empath is a hypersensitive person that can understand and resonate with other people, in a profoundly emotional way. They have the ability of "absorbing" the energies from their environments, good or bad, and they are caring, kind-hearted individuals.

Some traits that characterize an empath are: high sensitivity - they have a lot of heart but are easily hurt, highly intuitive, usually introverts, they have a tendency to absorb the emotions of others, they can get overwhelmed by noise, light, excessive talking or strong smells, they thrive in nature/quiet environments, and they need alone time in order to recharge.

The sensitivity of an empath is both a blessing and a curse. It makes them relate to people uniquely, but it also makes them living targets for energy vampires- such as the narcissist. An energy vampire can easily "eat away" the energy of the empath, leaving them tired and mentally disturbed. On top of that, a narcissist can effortlessly manipulate an empath into believing that they are worthless and undeserving of love.

Emotional vampires are very drawn to empaths because of their compassion and positive energy. They feed on these and thrive, while you are depleted and too tired to care for your wellbeing. If you find yourself in that list of traits listed above, then it's very understandable why you got in this situation. You are like a delicious ice-cream on a hot summer day for your abusive partner.

If you believe you are an empath, and you are able to *feel* the world, then don't fall into despair. There are beautiful things about being an empath. You have the capability to help other people. Also, your feelings and experiences are so intense that they give you a unique view of the world, that few people have. There is a lot of beauty out there, that only an empath can see.

The Cycle of Narcissistic Abuse

A relationship with a narcissist is, and will always be, abusive in nature.

However, what makes it somewhat harder to initially classify it as such is the fact that it does not follow the traditional formula of abuse in domestic situations, which was originally developed by Leonore Walker in 1979. Her model for the cycle of abuse consisted of three main stages: a tension-building stage - when one partner is extremely dominant and overly-demanding while the other complies; the violent episode - the point at which the victim tries to fight back or escape; honeymoon stage - the abuser shows to be remorseful and the victim forgives him/her in hopes of a better future, also this period gives the illusion of a normal relationship.

The cycle of narcissistic abuse has some similarities but, overall, it requires its own "model for domestic abuse" to better fit the situation. The recognized phases and patterns of narcissistic abuse are: Idealize, Devalue, Destroy, Discard, and Hoover.

Idealize

Before the narcissist can start their abuse, they need to entice their victim with positive emotions. This stage marks the beginning of the relationship, where the narcissist "love bombs" their partner and puts him/her on a pedestal. The "love bombing" manifests through excessive compliments, praise, attention, amazing dates, expensive gifts, and it has the purpose of making you feel infatuated and charmed. After some time from all these feel-good emotions, you naturally start to trust the narcissist and feel like you want to open up. Why wouldn't you? You are having such a great time together. When the darker periods of the relationship start to occur later, it is this love-bombing phase that the victim will cling to and try to re-live with their abuser.

By opening up to the narcissist, unknowingly, you start feeding them the data and information they need to get into your mind and find your weak points. Everything you ever told them about your insecurities, past issues, doubts, they will remember and use them as weapons whenever they will want to put you down - in the next stage of abuse.

The way they act during this stage lets their partner believe that they are connecting on a higher level, triggering the "soulmate syndrome" which comes with an extreme emotional link that will be very hard to break. While the victim perceives this idealization stage as the basis and fundamentals for a relationship that's made to last, in the eyes of the narcissist this is nothing more than a game that ensures their next supply.

At the end of this stage, the narcissist begins to see their partner as a "regular human," because of their emotional responses or actions that they do not approve of, and slowly the partner falls off the pedestal.

Devalue

The devaluation stage is characterized mainly by verbal abuse, forms of bullying (humiliation, threats, smearing), and acts of betrayal from the narcissist's side. The relationship jumps from your partner being proud of showing you off and being associated with you to you becoming someone flawed. All of your positive characteristics that he/she has admired before are transformed by the narcissist into something negative. Now you are a smartass instead of intelligent, your confidence is labeled as being cocky - or narcissistic, and your love for yourself and positive body image becomes vanity.

They start to actively put you down and gaslight all of your insecurities by diminishing your worth and your accomplishments. Everything you managed to achieve in life will be diminished, and they will paint your future in a grim light, instilling doubt in your own capabilities and decisions. Blatantly speaking they will do whatever they can to stop you from doing anything that he or she might perceive as an attack on their superiority. At that point, they have their victim trapped in the spider web they created, and they use their power and influence over you to dictate what you should think, your beliefs, your dreams, your image of yourself, your life choices, and the people that should or should not be in your life.

Their control is so powerful that your whole perception on life flips on its head, leaving you traumatized and heartbroken. This verbal abuse and diminishing will not stop until they completely strip you out of your free will, actively destroying you, or better said, the *you* that you knew/were before him.

You need to understand that this phase does not begin as a response to you doing something wrong. The victim bears no fault into the way that the narcissist chooses to interpret their actions or words. And through this whole process, the victim is clueless. They don't understand what they have gotten into, they don't see the web of lies and deceit trapping them. The victim gets so emotionally tired of all the insults and verbal abuse that comes their way that they would do virtually anything to get back to the original phase of the relationship when everything seemed perfect. The partners of narcissists will cling so hard to these memories of a better time, and they will truly believe in their hearts that going back is possible.

Destroy

Meanwhile, the narcissist stays on its road to destroy you and strip you of any ounce of confidence you might still have in your body. They will treat you in a barely acceptable way, putting in the least amount of effort. Even compliments will be used as a double-edged sword that will seek more to hurt you than to soothe your already bleeding heart. By this point, thanks to their manipulation, you already become dependent on them to offer you validation and admiration. As they go on with the devaluation and destroying your very person, they will use this desire of validation that you have against you. Anything you do will be seen as bad, and you will never reach the high standards they set, no matter how hard you try.

Other weapons that the narcissist will use in this stage is accusations and blame-shifting. Whenever the victim tries to defend herself/himself or tries to make the narcissist take responsibility for the way their words affect you, they will flip the situation and make themselves the "victim." They will blame you for being overly-sensitive, not smart enough to understand what they mean. They will emphasize how different you two are, mostly by portraying you as inferior / not worthy of being in a relationship with them. The narcissist will compare its actual victim with his or her ex-conquers, representing them as better in any way that you are. They will accuse you of things that more accurately describe them than you, such as: being self-centered, being a narcissist, not being understanding of their feelings and needs, not doing anything for them.

Out of all the stages that define narcissistic abuse, devalue - destroy is the one that comprises most of the per se abuse. It is done carefully, in a cold and malicious way, as the narcissist uses all the data that he/she has collected from you in the "idealize" stage, in order to break you apart piece by piece. Their only reason for doing that is to feed their illusion of superiority in the only way that he/she can: belittling you. Their whole life purpose is feeling good about themselves, no matter what tactics they need to employ in order to do that, or what/how many people will need to be exploited to achieve that.

Discard

When the victim finally reaches breaking point and has had enough and demands to be treated in a better way, they will discard the victim, in the search for someone new to idealize and repeat the cycle. This can happen quite quickly. Quicker than you expect as the narcissist most likely has had other victims entangled in the web in the early stages without you knowing. Social Media makes it a lot easier for the narcissist to keep multiple partners at bay.

Hoover

If most of the abuse happens in the devalue and destroy stages, this is one that can make the victim go through serious emotional trauma. When a narcissist discards a partner, it's only temporarily. They will most likely return to try and get their ex back into a relationship with them, even if they might already be involved with other people. As long as the narcissist believes that he or she can gain something by having you back, they will do everything in their power to get you back, continuing the cycle of abuse until the victim is strong enough to break it.

The heartbreaking fact is that, even when they are being discarded and forgotten for weeks or months, victims of narcissistic abuse will accept to give the relationship another try. It's not just the fact that they become addicted, but the victim finds it very hard to re-adjust back to their old life without the narcissist. Having parts of their identity stripped away, and their confidence at its lowest point makes going back into the world of dating and meeting new people seem incredibly daunting and scary. The loneliness and depression felt can be so deep, that it's almost impossible to resist when the narcissist attempts to "hoover" them, in the form of a text, call or Facebook message for example. The victim might get back together with the narcissist even if she/he was the one that initiated the break-up, and not the narcissist. That's just how powerful the influence of a person that has NPD is on a person with low confidence and self-worth.

The victim needs to understand that this attempt to get back together does not come out of feelings of love, concern, or the compelling need to re-connect. The narcissist will hoover their victim because they enjoy the feeling of power they get from it. It feeds their ego to know that they can get you back, whenever they want, as it shows how much control and power they have over you. They feel good knowing that they always have a backup supply to come back to, whenever they have needs to be catered to, and they will shamelessly do that even while actively pursuing other people or being in other relationships - especially if that other partner does not supply enough admiration/attention. The victim needs to understand that their relationship with the narcissist was never about love, not in the narcissist's perspective. Their sole purpose for wanting you back is to get something and to feel good about how they can bend people to their will. They don't miss the victim, because they are unable of having such strong feelings. The more people trapped in the narcissist's web, the better for them. Any action they employ is only for their gain and benefit. Love was never and will never be in her/his mind.

Fundamentals of Narcissistic Abuse & Cognitive Dissonance

In both the traditional cycle of abuse and narcissistic abuse, there are stages of rising and falling tension. The period of idealized/perfect relationship ends abruptly after an incident which triggers a violent episode, in traditional abuse cases or the beginning of the devaluation stage, in narcissistic abuse. In the latter case, there are multiple incidents of abuse in the devaluation stage, which will culminate with the narcissist discarding the victim, at least for some time. The moments of falling tension are characterized by the honeymoon period in traditional abuse cycles and by the hoovering in narcissistic abuse. In both models of abuse, the abusers will try to promote positive bonding (for example, the narcissist puts a temporary stop to devaluation and goes back to idealizing its victim) which makes it hard for the victims to escape the relationship. And so, the cycle begins again and repeats itself until the partner of the abuser puts a stop to it.

Christine Hammond, a mental health counselor, proposed a different model for the narcissistic abuse cycle, which focuses on the motivation of the abuser. It serves as a further way to differentiate traditional abuse from narcissistic abuse, and it offers a closer look at the dynamics of a relationship with a narcissist (which is solely driven by the narcissist's needs and desires). Hammond concluded that, at some point in the relationship, the narcissist begins to feel threatened by their partner. Remember that narcissists have very frail egos, and they might feel attacked by words and actions which have no ill-meaning behind them. When the narcissist perceives the "threat," that's when the abuse starts. They then proceed to devalue their partners, all while victimizing themselves, and, by the time the partner is deprived of any positive characteristics, the narcissist goes back to feeling superior/powerful. So, the model of abuse goes as follows: the narcissist feels threatened - the narcissist abuses their partner - the narcissist plays the victim - the narcissist feels superior/empowered.

Hammond's model for narcissistic abuse also highlights the different reasons for which victims go back into the relationship. In traditional abuse cases, the abusers actually experience remorse, and they convince their partners to offer them another chance with promises of change, which triggers the start of another honeymoon period that makes the victim think that the abuse is over. The victims of narcissistic abuse also hope that their partners would revert back to that initial phase of their relationship, but they are "forced" to stay in the relationship by the narcissist's methods of manipulation and victimization. Narcissists experience no genuine feelings of remorse, and their only motivation from getting back a partner is to satisfy their needs further.

In the traditional model of abuse, it has been noted that the abuser actively tries to keep the relationship going, even when the partner is aware of the toxic cycle they are stuck in. Narcissistic partners don't care if the relationship holds or not, and they only "fight" to keep a victim hooked to feel powerful over someone else and to continue using the said person. Also, the victims of narcissistic abuse are rarely aware of the toxic cycle that's part of their relationship. The narcissistic abuser has so much power over its victim that he or she feeds their partner their point of view, shifting the blame and making their partner oversee their wrongdoings. Victims of narcissistic abuse experience a type of "abuse amnesia" in which they forget all the negative feelings and thoughts they had for their abusive partner, a result of the narcissist's manipulation and constant abuse.

Victims of narcissistic abuse also suffer from cognitive dissonance. Most people require their behaviors and beliefs to be consistent. When a belief has been held firmly for quite some time, and then new evidence challenges this belief, it causes disharmony and great pain. The longer the belief has been held, the harder it can be to break. The victim can either choose to 'turn a blind eye' to this new evidence, holding onto the original belief OR respect the new evidence, break the initial belief and accept the pain to their identity.

In the first months of the relationship, the victim is so impressed and infatuated with the narcissist, utterly unaware that the emotions they are developing, are to a false identity; A mask. After some time, when the phases of devaluation and discard begin, and the mask slips off, it is hard for the victim to respect this new piece of evidence. It is much easier for the victim to continue believing in the false narrative holding onto the good emotions felt in the idealize phase rather than acknowledging the new evidence and change of behavior from their partner.

Acknowledging the reality that you fell in love with a 'person' that does not exist is excruciatingly painful. It can take many years for the victim to finally accept this as a reality, and in some unfortunate cases, the victim will refuse to accept this completely. During the cycle of abuse, the victim is continuously in a state of hope that their relationship will revert back to those 'perfect days,' replaying the positive shared moments experienced in their head. This, along with the fact that they are tricked into feeling responsible for the failed relationship, makes it very hard for the victims of narcissistic abuse to officially escape, prompting them to accept the narcissist back into their lives whenever he or she is hoovering them.

Main ideas about narcissistic abuse:

- It is preceded by a period in which the relationship is exciting/perfect.

- It starts when the narcissist perceives something that the victim did/said as a threat.

- The partner of a narcissist has no fault in triggering the abuse as narcissists have a warped way of perceiving reality, and the tendency of making everything personal.

- The narcissist uses manipulation to make themselves the victim of any situation that might put them in a bad light.

- The forms of abuse a narcissist will employ are: verbal, mental, and emotional.

- A narcissist will discard their partners whenever they feel that they are fighting back or when they no longer receive the admiration/love/monetary gain/sexual services they require.

- A relationship with a narcissist is never truly over after a break-up. The abuser will try to come back either to make themselves feel empowered by the control they have over you or because their new supply is not satisfying all their needs.

- Victims of narcissistic abuse have a hard time

escaping the relationship because the reality of falling in love with a false identity is too painful to accept. Their confidence and self-worth is depleted; they feel guilty about the break-up, they are prone to forgetting and overlooking the abusive episodes/negative characteristics of their narcissistic partner; and co-dependent tendencies make it very difficult to fight off this addiction when the narcissist keeps trying to get back into their lives.

- A narcissist never misses their ex-partners, and they don't feel remorse for their actions. The only reason they try to get back into a relationship is to continue using that person to satisfy their needs. In a narcissist's heart, there is no room for love.

The Narcissists Arsenal

A narcissist has many weapons in their arsenal when it comes to getting what they want out of a relationship.

Love bombing

Something that we have already touched on before. Love bombing is the first weapon that they use to 'reel you in.' Love bombing consists of a persistent wave of compliments, flattering comments, material proofs of affection, kind gestures, and touching. All this "show" that they make out how much they adore you has the sole purpose of making you believe that you may have found an amazing partner for a serious relationship. It may feel intoxicating in a good way, and, for people that have struggles maintaining a positive image of themselves and are co-dependent, it will offer a much-needed validation of their worth. Through love bombing, they manage to manipulate you not only into having romantic feelings for them but also to spend more time in their company, depriving you of your alone time or time that you'd typically spend with friends and family.

A narcissist will also be persistent in reminding you how "perfect you are for each other," and it's only thanks to their unusual charm that you are unable to see how weird that may be to say at the start of a relationship where you don't really know your partner that well. Love bombing basically serves the purpose of getting you where the narcissist wants: isolated from friends/family, in love with a charming "persona" that they manufactured to mirror your needs and beliefs, and forced into a relationship that's moving way too fast but unable to realize how smothering this sort of behavior is.

Manipulation

Narcissists will use multiple forms of manipulation. They know how to find your insecurities early on and then use them to gaslight you in the "devalue" stage. They victimize themselves always, feigning innocence at all costs, no matter how many lies they have to serve you or how much they need to distort the truth in order to get out of a sticky situation. Denial is in their DNA, so, whenever they are responsible for any bad situation, they will go to the moon and back to try and make you believe their perspective, never willing to accept the consequences of their actions/words.

Arguments and fights are also used by the narcissist to showcase his/her abilities to play victim, all while actively blaming you and diminishing you for things that they are actually guilty of. They will deny and repeatedly lie to keep alive the illusion of innocence, even when you confront them with solid evidence. Even at times when they might slip the mask a bit and show their true character, they will still be persistent in their trials of having you give them the benefit of the doubt, and thus, spinning the situation in their favor. It "helps" a lot that their partners are kind-hearted individuals that over-estimate the good in people and have the tendency of overlooking their negative traits.

But why do they employ the use of fights and arguments?

Logically speaking, couldn't that lead to a potential break-up if they go too far? Well, yes and no. Narcissists love to play with the mind and feelings of their partners. They take pleasure in getting any sort of reaction because in that way they get to suck out your energy (FYI: narcissists are frequently called energetic vampires) and, as a side-effect, they get to test how much power and influence they have over you. The fights will always start as a result of something that the narcissist did/said, and they will always end with the partner taking the blame/forgiving them. Either way, they will benefit both from stealing away your emotional energy and from playing around with your mind - something that helps them keep the illusion of superiority alive.

Projection

Another weapon that is often used by your regular narcissist is projection. It's a very peculiar and strange thing to employ if you take some time to consider it, as projection ultimately shows the flaws and bad side of the narcissist. In a way, by using projection, they "betray" their cover. In simple terms, projection is a defensive mechanism that is characterized by accusing others of something that you are/have done. This is very apparent during arguments or fights when the narcissist will place on you all the bad/negative characteristics that they have or any bad actions that they did or would do, even if those could never truly characterize you. They basically take all of the emotions, characteristic traits, thoughts, flaws that they have and are not comfortable with, and they "give" them to you, so *they* won't be forced to deal with them.

Narcissists are unable to take responsibility for anything, so it is in their nature to shift the blame onto someone else. That's what projection is: a combination of blame-shifting and misdirecting feelings/thoughts. Instead of accepting them as their own, they reflect them on others to protect their frail grandiose image of themselves. They are also managing to distract you from seeing the truth, and they make you claim responsibility for something that they are guilty of. Good examples of projection are the narcissist being overly jealous and convinced that you might be cheating on them, all the while they are the ones that are seeing other people behind your back. Or the narcissist might badmouth someone and critique them for the way they look or for a character trait that they also possess. For narcissists, projection is crucial for their survival, as it allows them to assess their negative feelings/traits/habits without having to actively deal with them or accept them, protecting their false self from harm.

Language

Now let's speak about language and communication. Even those are not safe from the corruption of a narcissistic individual. It becomes a full-blown weapon of war made to protect themselves at all costs and used to harm others. They use communication merely as a way to deceive, hide, and evade blame, but they don't actually transmit any messages. They have strangely mastered the art of speaking a lot without saying anything - something they will mainly use to monopolize conversations or confuse partners when they confront them with evidence of misconduct. Language serves the purpose of belittling others and keeping a narcissistic supply nearby. They never use it to speak *to* people, but rather to speak *at* them, lecturing them on senseless subjects and camouflaging their own vile character. The way that a narcissist uses language is almost impossible to understand as it makes no sense.

Shmuel Vaknin, the author of "Malignant Self Love: Narcissism Revisited," does an excellent job of describing how a narcissist uses language. Let's take a normal conversation for a second. We, as human beings, tend to communicate with one another by transmitting information. This information may be right or wrong, subjective or objective, emotional or scientifical, that does not matter. The core of communication is *transmitting*, in order to potentially build relationships or just for the sake of human contact.

In this aspect, narcissists are very different from regular people. They don't use communication as a means of transmitting anything. The information they blast is empty of any substance. For them, language is just a weapon of manipulation, a means to defend themselves against critiques or opinions that differ from their own or a way to critique/diminish others. Agreements or commitments mean nothing more than a momentary intent to a narcissist.

The narcissist will often lose himself/herself in loop-hole type conversations, where they say the same things all over again, and they often contradict themselves although they seem blissfully unaware of that discrepancy. Many of their statements will defy logic and reality, and any attempt at correcting them will get their conversation partners nowhere. Logic and consistency simply do not define the conversation pattern of a narcissist.

So what are the elements to look for in a conversation with a potential narcissist?

- statements that defy logic/reality

- repetition
- sentences that remain unfinished
- saying a lot without actually saying anything
- a one-sided show that resembles a preach or speech more than a conversation

Shmuel Vatkin also focuses on the fact that narcissists will generally avoid any serious or meaningful conversation, preferring to play out their own fake narrative in their minds in which everyone adores them. Instead of seeing people as they really are, they will create projections of them, who, in their mind, are made to serve him or her and cater to his or her needs. Whenever the narcissist gets into a situation in which the real person does not comply with his/her mental image of them, he/she will be very surprised and will refuse to accept reality. For example, the narcissist might word his/her surprise over the fact that his/her son did not follow them as an example, as a matter of choosing careers, not being aware that the child in question never had any intention to do so. Or the narcissist might say that his wife changed and no longer listens to him, not realizing the fact that she only did so out of the fear/desire to save the relationship, not because she adored him.

If we are to believe Shmuel Vatkin, a conversation with a narcissist is never a real option, because you can't communicate if both parties are not interested in doing so. A conversation will always be just a one-sided act, in which the truth will most likely be distorted.

Cognitive dissonance

Last but not least, in our list of the weapons that a narcissist uses/relies on, we have cognitive dissonance. I've mentioned it briefly before, but now we are going to go a little bit deeper into it and see how that aids the narcissist in his/her quest to brainwash their victims. The idea behind cognitive dissonance is that, whenever we are faced with something that is not consistent with what we believe or when we are confronted with new information regarding something that we feel strongly about, we unconsciously find a psychological way in which we make said thing seem consistent. The most striking examples of that are apocalyptic type cults or conspiracy theorists that will keep on believing something despite an incredible amount of factual evidence against it.

Now, cognitive dissonance is a frequent normal phenomenon that we all have to deal with on a daily basis, whenever we are faced with information that may question something that we believe/think highly of. Because this is an unconscious phenomenon, we will meet people that are very careful with their health but indulge in bad behaviors such as drinking or consuming dangerous substances, or people that always boast about needing to save money despite them buying useless things on a regular basis.

When we add a narcissist into the mix, cognitive dissonance goes to a whole new level. The narcissist will constantly force their partners to go over the information and choose what to believe. They are fully aware of how difficult it may be to have two separate images of them: the charming person from the beginning of the relationship and the selfish partner. And they use this "discomfort" to get their way. When a person has cognitive dissonance, their initial beliefs regarding their partner are very resistant to change as they have developed a plethora of secondary beliefs on top of them, which basically comprises the way they have been living their lives. This foundation is so strong that it would take a lot of psychological effort to change it and accept a conflictual view. For people that are in relationships with narcissists, they form this strong belief in the first stage of the relationship. They become fully convinced that their partner is "the one," and no matter how much their partner changes and how far he/she goes from their original "persona," the victim will constantly hold onto this belief that there must be an explanation for the strange behavior. In other words, they will find excuses or reasons, no matter how illogical they might seem, in order to keep that initial belief, that they have a good person next to them, intact.

Bree Bonchany, a therapist that works with victims of narcissistic abuse, explains how this initial belief forms, and how victims cling to it, despite constant proof that their partner is not who they thought:

"The love-bombing of the idealization stage of a toxic relationship sows the initial seeds of cognitive dissonance. The narcissist fakes being the ideal partner by saying and doing all the right things. They pretend to be everything we ever dreamed of and shower us with promises of perfect and eternal love. We are conned into believing the narcissist is the best partner we've ever had and the most wonderful person on the planet. We trust their promises and believe they're able to love wholeheartedly, and without limits, in the same way, we do.

We fall madly in love, and our brains become drenched in a potent cocktail of love-bombing, and the pleasure-inducing chemicals, that are released by neurotransmitters in our brains, when we are in love. This potent cocktail is what germinates the seeds of cognitive dissonance, which were planted in our minds, during the idealization stage.

By the time the devaluation stage occurs, and the narcissist's behavior begins to deviate from the way they first acted, our positive regard for them, and our beliefs about their good character and intentions, have grown like weeds that have permeated, and become firmly rooted throughout our minds."

According to Bonchany, the confusion created by the two opposite beliefs causes mental stress, and we choose to stick to our original beliefs as a way of protecting ourselves because we are not mentally and emotionally ready to accept reality. We do that by denying the new information, finding explanations for it or simply ignoring it. Sometimes we may even take the blame in an effort to protect the relationship, or we actively choose to live "in the past" when the narcissist was still that lovable, charming person - refusing to see the monster he/she has become.

The consequence of this is that the victim suffers a detachment from reality. The inconsistencies in behavior, statements, and beliefs are so severe that the person subjected to them might feel like they're going crazy. Any mentally healthy person is not psychologically prepared to face a relationship with a narcissistic individual. The victims become so brainwashed that she or he starts to actually believe that they do not know how a relationship should be and how it should work, ultimately letting the narcissist take the wheel. Whenever the belief that his/her partner might not be good for them creeps in, a memory of better times will also pop up in their minds, stopping victims of narcissistic abuse from making any definite decision regarding the relationship.

Cognitive dissonance is the worst weapon that a narcissist can use because it has multiple negative effects:

    1. It makes the partner develop loyalty towards the narcissist. Also known as 'Stockholm Syndrome.' A

condition in which the victim develops a psychological alliance with their captor during captivity.

2. It allows for partners of narcissists to sustain abuse without realizing it.

3. It makes victims of abuse vulnerable to being used by the narcissist, and it keeps them in a constant state of bad mental health.

4. It has long term effects that will haunt victims of narcissistic abuse a long time after the relationship is over, leaving them unable to understand what has happened to them and prone to getting themselves in similar situations.

I hope this chapter shed some light on how resourceful narcissists are and why it is so easy to fall into their trap and stay there. Understanding what you were/are up against is one of the first steps towards escaping and rediscovering yourself.

Narcissist's Language

Narcissists are skilled manipulators, and part of that is thanks to their ability to play with words and their meanings. To really get a grasp on how the mind of a narcissist works, you need to understand their language. Nothing is as it seems. So, let's look at some usual phrases and see what the actual message behind a narcissist's compliments, apologies, and overall speech is.

Compliments

"**You are so much better than my ex. He/she was crazy!**" - "In reality, it is my fault that we broke up, I was the problem. But you don't need to find that out, because I'm never guilty of anything. If you leave me or we break up, I'll say the same about you."

"**You are my soulmate**." - "You are my target right now, and I'll say anything to get you to like me. I'll keep love bombing you with compliments until you give up and accept me in your life."

Apologies

"**Sorry you feel that way**." - "I don't believe there is any reason for me to apologize, but I will do it to shut you up. I am never wrong / I can never do anything wrong. It's always your fault for being a normal person and displaying emotions / reacting to my abusive behavior."

"**It's not going to happen again / I promise not to do it again.**" - "I will absolutely repeat this action/behavior that upset you. If you catch me in the act again, I'll lie and come up with excuses, just to keep this relationship going a little longer. Never believe my promises."

Complaints

"**You are so emotional/dramatic/sensitive/insecure.**" - "I need you to think that your way of behaving is wrong and that your reactions are over the top, so I can get away with my actions/behavior. In reality, I like to stir up drama and to gaslight your insecurities, to make you more manageable. I am also overly sensitive to criticism, and I will over-react whenever my superiority is being questioned."

"**You take everything too seriously / You have no sense of humor.**" - "I use humor as an excuse to insult you and make you feel less of a person. I take pleasure in deliberately hurting you and then pretending that it was all a joke."

"**You're such a smartass/nerd/know it all**." - "You are smarter than me, and I don't like that. I always need to feel superior in any way, and your intelligence threatens me, so I have to make you feel bad for being correct/smart."

"**You never do anything for me!**" - "That's far from the truth, but I want to make you feel like a horrible person, even though I am the one that never does anything for you. I need to feel morally superior to you, so I'll undermine your kindness."

"**We never have sex / My ex loved to (*a sexual act that you are uncomfortable with*), but you never want to try** it." - "I want you to feel bad for not satisfying my every wish and desire. I'm blatantly lying about my ex, in order to get you closer to complying to my every whim. There is a chance that you will feel guilty enough to overstep your boundaries, which no one should be forced to do."

"You are such a narcissistic person / You only think about yourself." - "I want you to feel toxic and guilty in order to put myself in a good light and keep the relationship alive. In this way, I can go on abusing you, without having to answer for my actions. I am the narcissistic one, and I will always put myself first, no matter what. I will do my best to manipulate you into believing that you are the crazy one in this relationship."

Using "break-up talk" as a means of keeping you hooked

"You are too much for me." - "I can't handle your emotions even though I am actively provoking you, any chance I get. Your emotions are annoying to me, and I want you to believe that you're over-reacting."

"We are just so different / We have nothing in common." - "I lack any ability to empathize, and I am not compatible with anyone. But I need you to feel like the problematic one in this relationship. I want you to feel bad for having feelings and human reactions, even though I am the one that affects our relationship."

"Let's take a break." - "I need to make you feel insignificant and to crave my attention while I go about my life finding possible targets and not caring about the pain I'm putting you through. You will want me back anyway."

"I'm done." - "You'll never get away from me. I will always come back when I feel like it. I have no intention of breaking up, but I'm in a situation where you want to make me accountable for my words/actions, and I need to get out of it. I will never take responsibility for my actions/words, and I will find ways to pin the blame on you and make you feel like you or your opinions don't matter. If we ever break up, I will try to get back to you and ruin you as much as I can."

"Let's just be friends with benefits." - "A break-up is inevitable, but I still want to have a way of coming back into your life later on and continue my abuse. Or, I know you love me, but I want to lower your expectations while I wait to find someone else."

Manipulative/Controlling phrases

"My ex would never do that." - "I want you to feel inferior and to question the way you are acting/reacting. Your behavior is normal, and my ex probably reacted the same, since I'm not with them anymore, but I don't want you to think that you are entitled to acting/reacting that way. You need to feel like the odd one out, the guilty one, so I can get away with my behavior."

"She/He is just a friend." - "I need a backup plan to satisfy my needs, be it monetary or sexual, while also making you feel insecure. I feel so powerful knowing that I make you question your worth by having this 'friend.' If things go wrong with you, this 'friend' is my next target."

"I don't want to have sex with you / I don't care about sex." - "I want you to feel undesirable and unable to fulfill my desires/fantasies/standards. It will allow me to get away with looking for other sources for sexual gratification. I also enjoy making you feel insecure as it strengthens my power over you."

"You should be careful with the people you put your trust in." - "You have people in your life that love and support you, and I don't. I want to ruin your relationship with other people out of sheer jealousy and to further establish my influence over you. The lonelier you are the easier I can manipulate you."

"Nobody cares about you or your accomplishments." - "You need to be dependent on me so I can be the superior one. There are too many people caring about you, and I want you to question their honesty and reasons. I want to isolate you, so you have no support. You only need me."

Narcissists know how to plant the seed of doubt in your brain. They use words as weapons and they will always attempt to diminish you, either by making hurtful jokes or by painting you as the "bad guy." How many of these phrases are familiar to you? Are you able to see the bigger picture now that you have a "translation" of what your partner was actually saying? You can see how these 'digs' at your self worth over a long period of time can really affect you.

The main ideas that you should take away from this chapter are:

    1. Never let anyone establish your worth as a human being.

    2. In fights/conflicts, guilt is shared between the participants. Always be wary of people that never take responsibility for their actions and constantly play the victim.

3. Don't let anyone disconnect you from your support network. Your friends and family would never think bad of you or judge you.

4. It's perfectly normal to have emotions, that doesn't make you overly sensitive.

5. Maintain your boundaries and never let someone force you out of your comfort zone in any situation, especially in sexual ones.

6. In a healthy relationship, no one is superior. You are equal human beings that work together towards a better future and a happy life. Differences are fine and should be embraced, not used against each other.

7. Excuses and apologies mean nothing if a person is not actively trying to better themselves and not repeat the same mistakes.

Hardships of Escaping an Abusive Relationship

We've talked about what narcissists are, how they choose their victims, how they make you lose control over your life, and how we can characterize narcissistic abuse. But, one more thing needs to be set in stone before we start on the healing journey, and that is how exorbitantly hard it is to escape an abusive relationship.

The world is full of people that share their opinions on sensitive topics without having any factual basis on what they are actually talking about. We live in an era of information, but, ironically, we are more misinformed than ever. Which is why people still ask themselves why men or women that are in abusive relationships don't just leave and never look back? Why are they accepting to be treated badly, and even go as far as to protect their abusers? That is the toxic mentality of blaming the victim, for a situation that is incredibly complex, on a psychological front. And the bad part is that a lot of the victims of narcissistic abuse already blame themselves for the situation they went through and for the failed relationship.

It's enough to just take a look back at one of the previous chapters in this book, "The Narcissists Arsenal," to at least start to understand why victims feel compelled to stay. Narcissists have so many tactics and weapons that they ruthlessly use, and they also know how to choose the perfect targets. They purposely go for people that are very "in tune" with the feelings of others, that have a tendency of putting the needs of others first, that are generally trusting and kind, with low self-esteem and have high traits of co-dependency. It's like using nuclear weapons to take down a rural village full of farmers, with little to no knowledge of wars. Narcissists are predators that feed on other people's energy and emotions. They are first-class manipulators that plan their every move and do whatever it takes to get what they want. How is anyone supposed to be prepared for something like that? For an encounter with a movie-like villain that knows exactly how to get you hooked?

Let's backtrack a little and give a summary of how someone becomes the victim of a narcissist.

The unaware victim is idealized/love-bombed by a charming, well-spoken individual, and ends up falling in love with a mask, an illusory image that the narcissist displays. The abuser keeps up the facade of love and appreciation until they are confident that their partner is fully invested in the relationship - only then the true character of the narcissist starts to show its ugly sight. Many of these victims get into the relationship as strong-willed, independent people, but they are slowly stripped of any positive traits. Their empathy and kindness are used against them, and the constant manipulation tears them apart. The power of the relationship is in the hands of the narcissist, and the love and affection are one-sided. The abuser slowly chips away at their victim's self-worth, exploits them in order to satisfy their own needs and manipulate their way out of any confrontation. The narcissist never feels remorse and avoids any responsibility for his/her actions/words, projecting anything "bad" onto their victims. As the abuse intensifies, the victim starts feeling hopeless. They are always emotionally assaulted, verbally abused, and practically terrorized on a psychological level until they have only a few choices left: to deny the abuse, to minimize its significance, to rationalize the whys behind their partner's behavior, or to find a way to revitalize the relationship and improve their "bond" with the abuser.

I've already dabbled in codependency and how codependent tendencies can trap you in an abusive relationship. But, even in the absence of codependency, the abuse itself has a very traumatizing effect on the brain, which can tie a victim to its abuser, both psychologically and organically (referring to biochemical reactions such as the secretion of neuro stimulants like dopamine and serotonin). This "connection" is known as trauma bonding. No matter how strong-willed a person is or was prior to the relationship, in time, as the abuse escalates, they can show signs of trauma bonding, post-traumatic stress disorder, or complex post-traumatic stress disorder - a prolonged and more extreme version, as a matter of symptomatology, of PTSD. Severe chronic abuse and trauma will have a life-changing effect on anyone, no matter how tough they think themselves to be. And that's an accurate way to describe a relationship with a narcissist: constant severe abuse.

If we are going into the biology of trauma bonding, it all goes back to our inborn need to rely on someone else, for survival. Even after years of evolution, survival still stays at the core of human attachment, which is why we want a partner that makes us feel secure, protected, and cared for. When we find a person that, we believe, can provide what we need, our brains release oxytocin, also known as the "love hormone." We are wired to turn to a person we see as a caretaker (a parent, sibling, friend, partner) whenever we feel threatened by something. But, when the threat (abuser) also happens to be a caretaker figure, trauma bonding develops. Regardless of the abuse, we are unable to stop feeling linked to that person. Whenever the victim starts seeing the contradictions between the actions of their partners (care mixed with abuse) they try their best to rationalize them, which only further strengthens the bond. Especially when the abuser is a narcissist: they know how and when to push your buttons, and they have the tendency of twisting the reality of the victim until it starts seeing things from the abuser's perspective. The bond is also harder to break because of the narcissist's habit of hoovering their victims, whenever they please.

The effects of traumatic bonding vary from obvious to subtle and hardly noticeable. A very general effect of any abuse is the overproduction of cortisol. This hormone that is normally produced whenever we face a stressful situation can be very damaging if it goes over the usual marks. It can cause anxiety, damage the immune system, and negatively impact our blood pressure. Besides hormonal issues, traumatic bonding can also cause depression, sexual dysfunction, PTSD, and a slew of other health issues such as asthma, or fibromyalgia - characterized by muscle pains, fatigue, and mood issues.

There are other factors that make it harder on victims of abuse to break free from their abusers, which are: the inability to perceive that the relationship is toxic, the fear of starting from scratch with another person, the power that the narcissist has over their victims may be close to impossible to overcome, the belief that their partner might change, the misconception that they are in some way responsible for the behavior of their partner, or there might be other things or aspects of their life that link them to the abusers (monetary dependency, having a family with them, etc.).

Ambient abuse can also be put on this list, as it is a subtle, stealthy abuse that the victim most probably won't notice until it's too late. It is considered as one of the most dangerous forms of abuse, especially because of its ambiguous nature.

To end this chapter on an interesting note, here is the perspective of a self-aware narcissist, H.G Tudor, who seeks to help victims understand what has happened to them:

"You fell in love with an illusion. You fell hard and deep for something which never existed. The golden days that we created together were the twisted reflections of my manipulative hold over you. I know how anxious you were to try to recover the golden period. I know that my silence, my verbal violence, the cheating, and the lies, my perfidious control of you was brutal, malicious, and devastating. I understand that the whole avalanche of manipulative techniques I applied to you, in savage wave after wave crushed your self-esteem, mauled your sanity, and shattered your world. This brutality was nothing compared to the aftermath.

For now, you have slipped away from my tight, choking grip.

Memory after memory stirs from within, an endless loop of 'best of' moments that you want to stop remembering but you cannot. It hurts yet you still want to remember because even as the pain rises in your chest, you still feel the flicker of your love for me and you still cherish that.

The one lingering, torturous pain that still sits deep within you is the knowledge that you were in love with an illusion. No matter how much you discuss it with your friends, the earnest hours with your therapist and the pile of books about healing that are stacked up beside your favorite chair, none of them help take away that awful aching.

You can manage the shame of being fooled. You take a strange pride in having given your all to such a despicable person because that is the person you are. Honest, decent and a provider of unconditional love. You do not want that to change. You do not want to lose the empathy for which you are renown.

Your head will eventually accept what happened, that you

were charmed, entranced and enchanted and you never stood a chance. That was why you were chosen. Emotionally, you will never lose that dull ache as you sit and reminisce about our time together and how wonderful being in love with me was. Your heart will never accept that it was not real.

That crack, that fracture, that tiny chunk that remains from your frenetic and devastating time with me shall always remain. It is through it that I can return as I slip, shadow-like into your heart through that unhealed wound. That is why we did what we did; so, we always had a way back in.

You will have to maintain that vigilance for the rest of your life. Our polluting influence, if ever allowed near you again, will creep and trickle through the hole that will never seal. You are consigned to a lifetime of wariness and maintain your defenses because that damage is permanent."

Breaking Free From a Narcissistic Partner: Strategies and Advice

By this point in our journey to better understand narcissistic individuals, one thing should be crystal-clear: there is no chance for a long-term relationship with a person that has NPD. Any "love story" with such individual will end up with heartbreak, shattered dreams, and maybe even years of your life wasted away.

Even when the victim is held tightly in the narcissist's grasps and is forced to accept the reality that he/she wants, deep down, they are aware of the hopeless situation they are in. No matter how hard you might try to deny the truth and rationalize the actions of a narcissist, in the end, it all boils down to the fact that you fell in love with someone that never existed. A charming, wonderful person that promised you the moon and the stars, and you, a kind-hearted individual with a lot of love in your heart to give, trusted him/her. The reality that your soulmate was "fabricated" by a sick, malicious person is absolutely mind-shattering and heartbreaking, for anyone that has to go through it. The trauma eats you up from the inside, even months after the relationship has ended, and the experience changes you in ways you never knew were possible.

No matter how strong-willed, independent, confident someone was before entering into a relationship with a narcissist, the experience steals all of these good things away from you, reducing you to a shadow of your old self, an empty shell that feels hopeless. Not even celebrities are safe from the grasp of abusive relationships. Reese Witherspoon admitted in an interview with Oprah, to have been involved in an emotionally abusive relationship at a young age, also adding that leaving the said relationship was the hardest decision she ever had to make. Stacey Solomon, the presenter of *Loose Women*, has as well been outspoken about her abusive experience, going as far as describing on the program how it changed her, "I was in an abusive relationship, and it makes you forget who you are. It made me feel like I'd never be the same person again. No matter what I do, I'll always be this weird version of myself. A part of me does begrudge that person for taking that away from me. If someone says something over and over again, it can embed in you."

Another famous example, that might come as a surprise, is actor Johnny Depp. He was in a physically and emotionally abusive relationship with actress Amber Hart, but, because our society is biased to believe that only men can be abusers, people believed his now ex-wife's lies, and he was blamed for months of being the perpetrator. Hart used his fame and money to propel herself up, and even proudly advocated as a member of the #MeToo movement. It took several hours of video evidence, multiple witnesses, hospital bills, domestic violence reports, and even Hart herself confessing to attacking her partner in two instances, to make the public accept the fact that Depp was the victim all along.

So, to reiterate my point, abuse can happen to anyone, regardless of gender or popularity. Nothing makes us immune in this world filled with wolves in sheep's clothing. It sounds scary and hard to accept, but this is the reality of it. You are not at fault for putting your trust in a mentally deranged person, because you had no way of knowing their real self at the time. And when you did start noticing the truth, you were already strapped in the horror ride of your life, with little to no way out in sight.

Unfortunately, the only way to put an end to narcissistic

abuse is for the victim to initiate the break-up, as soon as he/she realizes that their partner is a narcissist. Break-ups take a lot of time, resilience, strength, effort, will-power, and support. It will take every single bit of energy that you may have left, after the constant abuse in your relationship, and, even when the break-up is done, the effective escape is only halfway done. Keep in mind that victims are emotionally and psychologically addicted to their partners and thus, very vulnerable to hoovering attempts. You may have to go through this 'break-up' 20 odd times until you build up the strength necessary to reject any reconciliation attempts. As time goes by, you will become more and more powerful. However, the only way in which you can break-off the control that the narcissist has over you is by adopting a **No-Contact** stance (or a low/limited contact if that's not possible).

No-Contact is the only solution that prevents relapse into the abusive, intoxicating relationship, and it is the first real step towards getting back control over your life. Think of a relationship with a narcissist as an addiction. You know that it's toxic and harmful. Even if it provides pleasures (in this case small episodes of "love" that makes you feel validated), a long-term relationship could ruin you and destroy you as a person. You realize that it needs to stop, but addiction messes with our brain in such a way that it is very hard to put an end to it. And in order to escape that addiction, you need to stay free of that toxic substance that your brain craves, or in this case, that toxic person. That's why **No-Contact** should be your first step. Your mind and body need to "detox" in order to truly start healing. Every contact you have with the narcissist, post-breakup, is equivalent to you taking in a small quantity of that "drug" back into your system, which is why the danger to "relapse" is so high in these situations. That little dose will have you wanting more, and after a long, emotionally draining fight to leave them, you will have to fight again, and again to make sure that you stay on the right track.

"**No-Contact**" keeps danger at a safe distance as long as you have the power to implement it. However, each situation is different in its own way. If there are children involved, you can't deny them the right to have both parents in their life.

Even though I will go on to present multiple strategies of "escaping" an abusive relationship that might fit most cases, please take the time to find and pick the one that's most suitable for your current situation. Take into consideration how bad your relationship has become, your level of self-respect, and when you consider that enough is enough.

Cold turkey

This term describes the abrupt cease of substance dependence. Which means you are basically stopping all contact with your abusive partner, leaving no room for reconciliation - thus ceasing your addiction of being in a relationship with said person.

Just as it goes for drugs or other addictive substances, abruptly ceasing your intake will lead to secondary effects. You will miss your partner; be tempted to give them another chance; think about the good times and forget the bad ones; or have the tendency to blame yourself for the situation. It's important that you don't give in and keep avoiding any sort of contact with your ex-partner.

This strategy is most suitable for abusive relationships with an element of physical violence / extreme emotional abuse; and in which you don't have other things linking you to the abuser (a family, monetary dependency, co-owned properties).

Gradually stepping away

This strategy is best for situations in which you can't immediately stop all contact with your narcissistic partner (maybe you are living together or there is another situation that prevents you from going "no contact").

Be very careful when you start limiting your contact with the narcissist as he or she will notice and try their best to change your mind. They might go through another round of idealization and love bombing or start playing games with your mind- anything really, just to keep you from leaving and to keep control over you. Remind yourself that nothing that comes out of the mouth of a narcissist is ever true.

Stop rationalizing his/her lies and validating them as truths, they are counting on that.

Stop making excuses for their unnatural behavior and giving them the benefit of the doubt. His/her actions are not your responsibility. You should not have to bear the weight of his/her mistakes.

Be resilient and remember that you are only a minor character in his/her drama show. Your relationship is just a game they play, and nothing more. You don't deserve to be treated like that. No one does.

No going back

In this strategy, the victim does something drastic that for them would make it hard or nearly impossible to go back into the relationship because the consequences of doing that would outweigh the temptation.

This "drastic" action needs to have special meaning for you, and it could be something as simple as changing your Facebook relationship status or as hard as writing a "goodbye" heartfelt message (in which you can pour all of your emotions and cleanse your soul) to your partner, followed by a stern no contact stage. Another thing you can try doing is telling your family or your trusted friend that you have chosen to break things off and explain why (even if you do it in vague terms). The shame you would subject yourself to if you accept him/her back after "exposing" him/her to your close one, could be more than enough to keep your mind far away from fantasies of getting back together.

Breaking point

This is more of a natural response rather than a method per se. It literally means that the victim has reached their breaking point: they realized that they are in a cycle of abuse that keeps on looping and that their partner will never change. They have gone through with it so many times that they are simply too tired to keep ongoing. Your self-respect reanimates from this slumber, and you realize that you deserve better.

When reaching your breaking point, a good idea is to write down your feelings and thoughts, so you will have something to go back to, and re-read whenever you feel tempted to go back into the abusive relationship. Go full "no contact" and be strong. Focus on the future and all the good things that are going to happen from now on in your life. The past should remain a closed door.

Deal-Breaker Evidence

This particular method is an absolute last resort and is not going to apply to everyone. It works best for a relationship that is already pretty much destroyed but to which you are extremely attached and can't seem to let go. You've also done no-contact multiple times and keep relapsing.

The key element for this strategy is to have a strong suspicion that your partner is cheating but you are denying the signs that you see. This ties in with the cognitive dissonance that we mentioned earlier. You can see the peculiar signs but are not fully acknowledging them or don't want to explore further because if you happen to be right, it's going to cause a world of pain.

Before you do explore further, this must be your 'line in the sand moment.' You've most likely had other lines in the sand that have been crossed by your narcissistic partner, and you keep moving the line for them letting them get away with their bad behavior. If this is not the 'line in the sand,' what is? How far are you going to keep moving the line? Deep down, you MUST know within yourself that if your suspicion does turn out to be true, you will feel too hurt and heartbroken to continue clinging to the relationship.

You're most likely never going to get a confession from your abuser. Why would your abuser hand you back your freedom on a silver platter? They're not going to. These people do not feel remorse, guilt or empathy. They want to keep you entangled forever. So if you do decide to go down this road, your abuser's kryptonite is their phone and computer. Social media has made it very convenient for the narcissist to have multiple 'projects' on the go simultaneously.

Does your abuser put their phone face down on the table all the time?

Does your abuser act weird when they get a message from someone?

Does your abuser have the text preview removed?

Does your abuser always have their phone on silent?

Does your abuser let you know their password to their phone and computer?

Does your abuser turn off notifications when they are around you?

Does your partner have communication apps hidden in strange places on their phone?

These are things to take note of. When someone has something to hide, they act strange.

"When you tell the truth, you don't have to remember anything." So, when someone is lying or hiding something from you, they have to spend energy to maintain this lie.

If you do happen to find what your gut may have been telling you, let the emotions out. There is no shame in crying. Allow yourself to grieve and let this be the end. This was the final straw for you, and now you are set free, as you realize that from this point there is no way the relationship can go on.

Co-parenting with a narcissist

When kids are in the picture, it is very important to take into consideration ways in which you can continue to "parent" along with a narcissistic partner in a safe way that does not endanger them or you, for the matter. Going no-contact can be very difficult, especially if your children are still young and incapable of understanding that one of their parents is not behaving properly. Seek the help of a therapist to work up together how you can be a functional family and do what's best for your children.

A helpful suggestion that may work for you is getting a trusted mediator who essentially acts as a middle-man for you, and that way you are able to completely remove yourself from being contacted by your ex-partner.

Detachment

Detachment is the process that any victim of any kind of abuse needs to go through, for their own good. It means understanding and accepting that your partner is not good for you and will never be. In other words, it means *letting go*.

We can boil down detachment to four distinct stages:

1. Stop taking the blame for everything your partner does and realize they are not perfect. In this stage, you also come to the realization that the relationship will never be how you envisioned it, and you stop seeing your partner through rose-tinted glasses. Reality hits you hard.

2. In stage two, you are still emotionally attached to your partner, but you start experimenting a wide array of other feelings: frustration, anger, and resentment. You begin to fight back and stop complying to their every wish. This stage is marked by an abundance of conflicts, as a result to you fighting back, and by doubting everything that your partner says, no longer allowing yourself to be the puppet in his/her one-man show.

3. The third stage is centered around you and your "revival." You are starting to regain some of your confidence and respect, and you begin to actively plan your break up. Now you are able to see your partner for the abuser and monster that he/she truly is.

4. And lastly, the final stage is cutting all ties with the narcissist. You physically move away from your partner, and you keep all communication lines closed. From here on starts the time of healing and slowly rebuilding

yourself.

Just because these stages are presented in a logical manner, it doesn't make it any simpler to go from stage 1 to stage 4. It's way too easy to get stuck somewhere between stage 1 and 2, and therefore, allow yourself to enter a loop of endless temporary break-ups. You need a lot of will power and strength if you want to move forward.

I already presented some strategies that might help you break free from the influence of a narcissist, but let's now go through some general ideas and advice, coming from both specialists and from people that had to undergo the same process as you - victims that rose above their traumatic experiences and managed to re-discover themselves.

Your value as a human being can only be determined by you

A lot of victims spend months or even years of their lives trying to reach the high standards of their narcissistic partner, only to be told repeatedly that they are not good enough. People are not perfect, and they never will be. Everybody makes mistakes, but that does not mean that our value as human decreases in any way. Not being perfect does not certify abuse.

A narcissist knows exactly what your insecurities are and how to use them against you. They will try to make you addicted to their validation, giving them the power to put us down or lift us up. But in reality, the only opinion that should matter is your own. You are the only person that is allowed to assess your value as an individual. Trust your gut and your beliefs. Stay true to yourself. Respect yourself and acknowledge your achievements. No one should be allowed to rob you of your identity. If someone doesn't love you for the way you are and forces you to change, then you are better off without them.

You are good enough.

Feed your "escaping" thoughts

When you get to the point in which you realize that the relationship is not going anywhere and your partner is not the person you want to grow old with, you start thinking about breaking up. No matter what, keep thinking about leaving your abusive partner. You reap what you sow, so if you keep feeding your mind these thoughts, you will start gaining more confidence about your decision. And you will feel, deep inside, that it's the right thing to do.

Whenever you are in doubt, close your eyes and remember all the times in which your partner made you feel unhappy. All the excuses you had to make for them, to your friends, family, or other people. Remember all the times they did not take responsibility for their actions and blamed you instead. How much shame can one person take in before it destroys them on the inside?

Don't get charmed away by nice memories of times that are long gone. There is no future for someone living in the past.

Trust yourself

Victims of narcissistic abuse are in an environment in which they have to constantly explain their every word and action, getting to the point where they doubt themselves so much that they feel that their every decision is wrong. This is one of the reasons why it's so hard to leave. Even when they have the decision in their mind, they still counter-attack it with arguments, often fed by the narcissists into their mind, and they can't find a logical reason as to why they should trust themselves.

You don't need to answer to anyone, or to worry about whether or not your decision will turn out to be a good one. Someone times you just know, what's the right thing to do. You feel it in your heart before you pass it through your mental analysis. However, your partner is a cunning manipulator. They will try to chip away at your decision and make you feel doubtful by bombing you with whys and hows. To which it is perfectly acceptable to say, "I don't know." It will spare you the need to explain yourself in the face of a person that would never understand, and it also leaves a door open for future knowledge. A tiny hopeful glimpse of a better future is hidden between that "I don't know."

Get second unbiased opinions

When you are in a relationship with a narcissist you are unknowingly made to live in an almost alternate reality, created by your abusive partner. He or she constantly tells you what you should think or what you should do, leaving you with almost no space to think for yourself. And because he/she already made sure to isolate yourself from your friends and family, making sure you feel guilty whenever you go out with anyone besides him/her, you often have no one else to give you honest/unbiased insight on the relationship. Even when you do step up and see your friends/family, you might still protect your abuser and avoid putting him/her in a bad light, because that's how narcissistic manipulation works.

Asking for opinions from friends that you may have in common with your partner's is pretty much pointless. Most of them live in the same warped reality as you and your partner. In psychological terms, they are called "flying monkeys," a term which describes people that believe in a narcissist's fake persona and that are very open to participating in smear campaigns - something that a narcissist does post-break-up. In other words, you can't trust them. The best place to ask for second opinions is from a couple's therapist or just a regular therapist, that will listen to what you have to say and give you the full dissection of your relationship. Getting feedback from someone that is not in the loop of the narcissist is very valuable, as it will help you see your relationship for what it truly is - an abusive bond.

No one is special

Narcissists have this belief that they are unique creatures that grace the earth with their presence. And they will also make sure to make you believe that what you and him/she have is special and unique and that there is no one else in the whole entire world, better than you two. You need to understand the reason why he/she is feeding you that information: to make you feel isolated. If there is no one like you and him, then you have no one to turn to and ask for advice. No one to help you understand the situation you are in.

It's hard to see things from the outside when your mind is controlled by such a powerful individual. Even if someone else intervenes and tries to show you the true nature of your relationship, you will have a hard time believing it. You need to see it for yourself, with your own two eyes. And the only way to do that is through actively seeking information. Search for your deep dark worries regarding your relationship and you will find articles relating to narcissism. You will start putting two and two together. You will begin to understand what your partner is actually saying and why he/she is doing what they are doing. Understanding helps you break free from the illusion and see reality.

The truth is that no one is special, or more special than other wonderful people that are out there. The sole idea that there are others like you, is very comforting. You are not alone in your struggles.

Accept your feelings

As you break up with your narcissistic partner once and for all, don't expect a wave of instant happiness to come your way. Your bond with your former partner, as flawed as he/she was as a person, was strong. You had moments of happiness and sadness. After all that happened, you might feel hurt, confused, frustrated, and even angry at yourself for allowing this experience to happen.

The only way in which you can heal and move forward is by allowing yourself to go through each and every feeling. It's perfectly acceptable to grieve. Just think for a second about all the things that you have lost: a partner that you love despite everything, a part of you that you will never get back, months or years of emotional investment, maybe your hopes and dreams that your narcissistic partner discouraged you from pursuing.

The pain gets better in time, as you start to forgive yourself and regain your hope for the future. Grieving is the human thing to do, and it is not in any shape or form shameful. Allow yourself the time to handle your emotions in the right way. Re-connect with friends and family, you stopped seeing when you got into your relationship.

Smear campaigns

I've mentioned a little while ago "smear campaigns," so let's see what those are about. In an effort of trying to keep the abuse going, a narcissist will go out into the world and tell every single person you know, from your family to your friends, co-workers, basically anyone they can get in touch with, their version of the break-up. Because during the relationship, the narcissist pressed you to not share many details regarding your interaction with him/her, it is very easy for this malicious person to spread misinformation. They will slander you and blame you for every bad thing that happened in your relationship, smearing your name. This gossiping gets him/her the attention and sympathy she/he deserves (or at least thinks she/he deserves), while also making you out to be the bad guy - a clever way to pressure you back into the relationship and in their grasp.

Expect the smear campaign and don't get intimidated by it. You do not need to waste time trying to convince everyone who did what etc. The truth will reveal itself over time. Your friends and family will always value your word above anyone else's.

The narcissist's next victim

You need to truly understand the fact that narcissists always plan ahead. While being with you, they are already planting the seeds for their next "harvest." Having a supply is necessary for the narcissist's survival. Without people to leech off of they are nothing.

So, they always have multiple potential victims at hand, out of fear that your relationship with him/her will end, or in case they get "bored" with you. They have a backup "harem" - a group of women/men ready to satisfy the narcissist's needs, at their disposal. The advances of today's technology only serve as a helping hand for the predatory narcissist. Thanks to Instagram, Facebook, and other social networks, or dating apps such as Tinder, the narcissist has now the possibility to "sell" their perfect version of themselves. They get followers that admire them unconditionally, and out of these huge masses of adorers, there are bound to be a few that the narcissist can easily manipulate, by simply making them feel special. We see cases like this more and more nowadays. Women/men or even minors being swept from their feet by their idol, just for them to be used and exploited. It's hard to fight back when you have a person that you genuinely admire/look up to, that knows how to easily manipulate you and use that admiration to their benefit.

Besides "helping" narcissists find victims, studies show that the rise of social media might also contribute to the rise of narcissism rates in youths, giving them an audience that boosts their self-esteem over the normal limits and making them develop that false sense of entitlement, often considered as an early sign of NPD. However, these studies are still in a very early stage, and we can't say for certain that social media "popularity" increases the risk of developing narcissism.

The Healing Process

One thing that must be very clear in your mind is that recovery from narcissistic abuse is very tricky. It takes a lot of time and effort, and in truth, the pain that you feel inside never goes away completely. Sure, it gets muted by other feelings, and you become stronger, capable of dealing with it in better, healthier ways. And yet, it remains. A chapter of your life that you can't ignore or forget. Going into recovery and expecting to go back to your old self is wrong. This experience changed your life so much that you are simply unable to re-become that person. The old "you" is gone. And that's fine. You now get the chance to reinvent yourself, a new "you" that has become stronger and wiser, as a result of what has happened to you.

In order to heal from complex trauma, a person must work through the phases of trauma recovery (not to be mistaken with the popular "five stages of grief," which are not extremely accurate despite their usage in pop culture).

Stage 1

Also known as "The emergency stabilization phase," in this first stage, the victim is extremely confused. They made the decision or were forced to go "no contact" with their narcissist, and now they are doubting themselves. The memories of the abuse are still fresh in the victim's mind and are in a continuous state of overstimulation - something that is also happening because the narcissist might still be trying to get in contact with you through mutual friends.

For someone that went through daily, severe emotional abuse, being calm and relaxed is a foreign feeling. Their normality re-defined itself as "being abused" while in the relationship, and once that happens it's hard to realize what normality should really look like. The victim still feels as if she/he needs to answer to their abusive partner for whatever they do/say, and that makes them extremely vulnerable.

In this first stage, what a victim most needs are support and reassurance. They need people actively telling them they made the right decision and helping them build back their self-confidence and trust in their decisions.

Stage 2

This is the start of effective recovery. The victim starts getting their energy back, instead of being continuously sucked out of them - something that a narcissist does. The victim's personality and emotions start showing signs of coming back, albeit timidly.

However, this stage is also dangerous. As the victim starts sorting out their feelings, they start experiencing bouts of anger and frustration, both towards their abuser and themselves, for allowing the abuse to happen. If the victim falls into this trap of self-blaming themselves, she/he might slip right back into stage one, unable to move forward through the stages of trauma recovery. The victim needs proper support, meaning specialized individuals, not social media support groups or friends. Relying too much on such forms of support might eventually become a setback in a victim's recovery process. A therapist knows how to properly guide someone through understanding and accepting their feelings - this is the sort of support that a victim desperately needs!

Stage 3

By this point, the victim is doing great as a matter of recovery. They are on their way towards rebuilding their identity, even if their trauma still makes it hard for them to move on. In this stage, the victim might slip into the dangerous act of giving the narcissist too much credit or trying to come up with an excuse for his/her actions. Thoughts like "we are both to blame for the fact that our relationship did not work out" and "he/she is a victim too, is not his/her fault for being this way" are perfectly reasonable for a person that is overly kind and compassionate, but you must understand that they are not true. It is just the good heart of the victim trying to find reasons to justify the actions of a morally abnormal person.

Still, in stage 3, the victim starts building up their confidence, even though they still feel in a strange way compelled to get back in touch with the narcissist. Not for reconciliation, but for an explanation. They want closure, or deep in their hearts they hope that the narcissist has changed (they never do). Be extremely careful when you get to this point in your recovery. You must keep the "no contact" strategy going (unless you have a family with them or something else that binds you two) or you become vulnerable to falling right back into the cycle of abuse.

Don't forget who you are dealing with: a manipulator, a predator, an opportunist. Not a lover that misses you and wants you back. If you get to this point, I would recommend doing some extensive research on narcissists to better understand how they "function."

Stage 4

At this point, the victim is capable to look back at their abusive experience and analyze it in an objective manner, without getting emotional about it. Feelings of anger and confusion are long gone. All that's left is the bare skeleton of a failed relationship that was not your fault.

When you are in stage 4, you are very aware of your emotions, your internal transformation, and you might even help others that are in earlier stages of their recovery. Although you have managed to build back an identity from the ashes of your old self, there might still be times in which you will slip back into negative feelings regarding yourself and doubt your capabilities of making choices. This doubt and tendency to belittle yourself is just another effect of narcissistic abuse, although you may not recognize it as such. Remind yourself that you are not that person anymore - you have grown, and you have gone so far from the vulnerable individual that was just fresh out of an abusive relationship.

This just comes to show how deep and long-lasting are the effects of narcissistic abuse. Patience and resilience are key.

Stage 5

A victim of abuse that gets to this point is able to see things as they are. They know who they are: their limits and their strengths. They are able to assess their own value as humans and individuals, wiping clean from their minds the lies and depreciations of the narcissist.

When you recover from the abuse, you will have a deep

understanding of what it means to be in a healthy relationship and how one is supposed to look like. You know your worth, and you respect yourself enough to not let anyone else walk all over you and undermine you. You know how to stand up for yourself and demand to be treated right. Some degree of caution is still advised since narcissists, and other emotional predators are everywhere. You have already proven to be the sort of empathic, kind-hearted person that this nasty type of person is drawn to, so be very careful. It is true that you have become stronger and more aware of how to recognize this type of people before you get entangled with them. Yet, it's better to be safe than sorry.

Your future is in your hands

While it is good to be aware of these stages of recovery, they are still a theory. They tell you how your recovery is supposed to go, they tell you little to nothing about how you are supposed to get there, except for employing the help of a specialized professional to sort through your emotional issues.

During the relationship, the narcissist became the focus point of your life. You had spent all of your time either with them or communicating with them through cute texts and never-ending phone calls. You went on amazing dates that you will probably never forget for the rest of your life. All this happens in the idealization phase, but that stage alone does enough as a matter of isolating you from friends and family and keeping you away from chasing your dreams. Anything else, but the narcissist, became secondary in your life. Your work might have suffered along with your relationships.

But now, your focus should be coming back to your own person. Remember your goals and ambitions! Remember your habits and the things you used to do for fun! Go back to those and re-activate the dopamine - the hormone of happiness, in your mind. You don't need to rely on the narcissist anymore to offer you validation and pleasure. Engage in your favorite activities and take back your happiness in your own hands - something that will make it easier to maintain the no contact rule with your abusive partner.

Here are a few ways in which you can naturally increase your dopamine levels:

- Adopt a diet rich in proteins (turkey, beef, eggs, legumes, dairy) and low in saturated fats (such as butter, animal fat, coconut oil). Proteins are essential because amino acids found in them help with the production of dopamine, while saturated fats can negatively impact the dopamine system.
- Have an exercise routine as it improves mood.
- Make sure that you get a healthy amount of sleep so that your dopamine receptors don't lose their ability to work properly. A good sleep schedule ensures that your dopamine levels stay balanced.
- Take in some sunlight to boost both your dopamine levels and subsequently your mood. Be careful to not go overboard with it as excessive sun exposure could cause skin damage.
- Listen to music - it actually increases levels in the reward and pleasure areas of your brain.
- Have a discussion with a specialist and determine (through some blood work) whether or not your body is in need of vitamin supplements. For example, deficient levels of vitamin B or iron could negatively affect your dopamine production. If you want to go all-natural, you can get Vitamin B from meat, dairy products, peas, leafy green

vegetables, and eggs, while iron can be found in fish, turkey, broccoli, and spinach. Consult a nutritionist for more options if necessary.

Besides making sure that your dopamine levels are kept at optimum levels, there are other things that you should look out for when healing a traumatized brain. Firstly, you should know that a brain that has gone through trauma works differently than a healthy one. To put it in simple terms, a traumatized brain has its "thinking center" under-activated because the narcissist fed you what to think at all times; the "emotional regulation center" is also under-activated as it had to be, in order for you to sustain the huge amount of constant trauma; and the "fear center" is overly activated - for obvious reasons. A brain that is in this condition has difficulties with assessing information and with managing emotions, even if the person actively tries to calm down and take it easy when they feel overwhelmed. Getting your brain back to its original state is hard, and it takes a lot of time and repetition. You will require the help of a psychotherapist that specializes in trauma, and who knows how to use evidence-based methods that can produce positive changes in your brain.

Secondly, you will have to make some changes in your regular, day to day life. Learn/practice relaxation techniques, such as meditation, that deactivate the fear center of your brain. It will not only help you relax, but it also gives you the chance to focus on yourself and restore your self-image. It will aid you in forgiving yourself and accepting yourself, which is crucial for recovery. You can also try to practice breathing techniques, other types of self-discovery methods, maybe yoga - it would also offer a chance for meeting new people and getting in tune with your spiritual side.

And last, but not least, in order to help not only your brain but yourself to advance further on this recovery journey, there are some additional changes/things you should try or at least consider doing. It's nothing scary, don't worry. Some of these things will bring you a lot of joy, even if others might be a bit hard to do at first. Smother yourself with self-love, self-respect, and self-care in order to start feeling good about yourself again. You have been through a lot. The narcissist has scooped out an enormous amount of self-worth from you in an attempt to make you a serving slave to them. We need to refill your self-worth and get you feeling good about yourself again and there are many ways we can do that:

- Sit down and create a list of achievable goals, something you can work toward and look forward to. Think of all the things that you wanted to accomplish prior to the relationship or all the interests and passions that you have ignored while you were under the narcissist's influence. There should be at least a few things that pop in your mind. Just be careful to focus on achievable things - be mindful of what you can do and don't try to force your limits. Goals give you a purpose in life, and right now you desperately need one, to motivate you and keep you on track.

- Be physically active even if you are not the type of person that particularly enjoys sports. Besides improving your dopamine levels, physical activity also prompts your brain to secrete endorphins, substances that combat the cortisol that was overly produced due to stress. Choose a type of activity that you would truly enjoy, such as dancing - which has a lot of great benefits to it. However, try to consider first a sport/activity that can be done in teams or with a group of people, as it would be very beneficial for you to socialize. Especially with yoga, where most people are very positive and mindful of other people's feelings. It will help you fend off all that negativity that you have gathered from the traumatic experience.

- Get back in contact with the people in your life. This might be very hard at first because you will have to explain your situation and therefore, "expose" the true nature of your relationship. For you, this will be a bitter-sweet victory as it offers up a cocktail of emotions: shame, anger, relief, and gratitude. But you will be surprised to see that most of the people in your life were already aware of your hurting, but they either decided to not interfere or if they tried, you may have pushed them away. Trust your friends and family. They know you and the type of person you are. They will be there for you to support and love you in your time of need.

- To further expand on this point, be selective with the energy you surround yourself with. Yes, the narcissist may have shattered your boundaries in the past but it is time to rebuild these boundaries from the ground up. It is time to no longer tolerate an ounce of negativity or put-downs from anyone. By surrounding yourself with good energy and vibes only, you put yourself on to the fast track for a healthy recovery.

- Re-engage with your old hobbies that you had prior to the relationship, especially if they are creative or related to the outdoors. Writing, painting, and sculpting might offer you a way to express yourself, helping you re-define your lost identity and maybe get rid of some of that emotional baggage. Video games and reading gives you an entrance into a different world, one in which you can relax and have a good time. Physical activity keeps your body occupied while your mind roams free. Going on walks, hikes or treks gives you the opportunity to be in nature, which is known to be therapeutic for both our minds and our souls. If you don't want to re-engage with an older hobby then start a brand new one from scratch, be it creative or active. Even starting a new business could give you a great opportunity to focus your mind on something both positive and stimulating. Who knows? Maybe you'll even get a new career out of it.

- Escape for a bit from your everyday life. You've been through a lot. It's perfectly fine if you need to go away for some time, in a new exciting place to heal and recharge your depleted batteries. It could be a very refreshing experience to get in contact with a different culture, meet new people, and just explore the wonders that our beautiful world has to offer. Your mind will thrive in a new, exciting environment!

- Laugh as much as you can. Laughter is the ultimate medicine for both your mind and soul. It makes your brain secrete substances that make you feel good and it puts you into a good mood. Go out with your fun-loving friends, see your favorite comedy movies/TV serials, watch stand-up comedy shows, or do anything else that will put a smile on your face.

- Start reading empowering materials. Read self-development books that present motivational stories and good advice. If you feed your mind with positive, empowering materials, which is good-quality food for your brain, you are being proactive in helping your mind heal.

- And last but not least, go splurge on yourself. Get that massage you've always been meaning to get but never made the time for. Get that manicure. Buy that outfit you've always wanted to buy. Try that new hairstyle you've been thinking about getting. Let this be your own stamp of authority that you will not allow yourself to ever be walked over again and your self-worth is not something to be toyed with.

To end this chapter on a good note, here are some "healing affirmations" that you can use as tools to help you move away from the negative mindset that the abuse caused. Use them at the beginning of every morning to boost your mood, hope, belief, trust, and your self-esteem. By using positive daily affirmations, you are re-wiring your subconscious mind which in turn will result in a more desirable and positive reality.

"I am healing one step at a time."

"I am a good person, that deserves love, affection, and respect."

"I surround myself with positive energy only."

"I am worthy of the beautiful things the Universe has to offer me."

"I am open to the beautiful things the Universe has to offer me."

"I love myself."

"I surround myself with people who respect me and my boundaries."

"I am grateful for my friends and family."

"I am putting the past behind me, and I will focus on the present and future."

"I am making a priority out of my recovery."

"I can trust my mind and my instincts to lead me towards making the right decision."

"My boundaries are strong, and nothing can make me overstep them."

"My friends and family will always love and support me, no matter what."

"I choose to become a better version of myself each and every day."

"I continue to learn and educate myself."

"I am improving each and every day."

Conclusion

Here we are, at the end of it all. You now know what a narcissist is and how they "work."

They are unable of feeling "love" towards anyone else but themselves. They live for the sole purpose of having their needs and expectations met, and they are under the false belief that the world owes them something. A relationship with a narcissist is just a fancy way of spelling "emotional and psychological abuse" and nothing more. All the love, support, care, and empathy are one-sided, from you towards them. They leech off of you and feed on your adoration and insecurities. You are their tool and nothing more.

However, no matter how hard it may be, you can always escape. Despite what your abuser is trying to make you believe, you are still in control of your own life and choices. You can choose to leave. Why? Because you had enough. Because you are a human being and you deserve to be loved, respected, and taken care of. You deserve to get in return as much as you give. Have the courage to break off the chain! Your friends and family will be there to support you. Your mind and your heart will heal. You will be fine! But your life won't really "start" until you choose to go.

I have given you ways in which you can safely leave an abusive relationship. Whatever you may choose, remember that NO CONTACT is the best way to go if you have no deeper ties linking you to your abuser. No contact means no temptation. It means that you are protecting yourself from the possibility of ever going back to the cycle of abuse. The narcissist won't make it easy on you, by hoovering and trying to reach you in subtle ways, but don't give in. Every time he/she tries to come back, remember the way he/she made you feel - not at the start of the relationship but at the end of it. Remember the sadness, the pain. The shame of having to come up with explanations on his/her behalf. The frustration of taking responsibility for something they have done. And think about the future you want: your goals, your plans, all the things you want to try. All the people that will be there for you. Think about a future in which you can love and be loved back by someone that genuinely cares about you!

You deserve to be happy. You deserve to be loved. You are capable of making the best choices for yourself and you must trust your decisions. Recovery is hard but it will happen - with slow but confident little baby steps. You will never go back to being who you were *before*, but you have the power to decide who you are going to be. Have faith in your own abilities. Don't be afraid to ask for the help of others, both professionals and regular people. Support groups and friends will always be there when you need them.

You are a strong, wonderful, kind-hearted person. And you will be fine. Allow yourself the time you need to heal and take care of yourself!

I wish you the best of luck with your journey and recovery, and if you found this information in any way helpful to you and your situation, please let me know in the form of a review. It gives me great satisfaction to know that I have been able to help someone along their troublesome journey as I know how hard it can be to free yourself from the web of a narcissist. This will also help other victims out there desperate for a helping hand.

Thank you

www.ingramcontent.com/pod-product-compliance
Lightning Source LLC
Chambersburg PA
CBHW071436080526
44587CB00014B/1865